Executive Coaching with Backbone and Heart

Mary Beth O'Neill

Executive Coaching with Backbone and Heart

· ·

A Systems Approach to Engaging Leaders with Their Challenges

Jossey-Bass Publishers
San Francisco

Jossey-Bass books and products are available through most bookstores. To contact Jossey-Bass directly, call (888) 378-2537, fax to (800) 605-2665, or visit our website at www.josseybass.com.

Substantial discounts on bulk quantities of Jossey-Bass books are available to corporations, professional associations, and other organizations. For details and discount information, contact the special sales department at Jossey-Bass.

 Manufactured in the United States of America on Lyons Falls Turin Book. This paper is acid-free and 100 percent totally chlorine-free.

Library of Congress Cataloging-in-Publication Data
O'Neill, Mary Beth, 1953–
    Executive coaching with backbone and heart: a systems approach to
    engaging leaders with their challenges / Mary Beth O'Neill.— 1st ed.
        p. cm. — (The Jossey-Bass business & management series)
    Includes bibliographical references and index.
    ISBN 0–7879–5016–5
    1. Executives—Training of.   I. Title.   II. Series.
HD30.4 .O53 2000
658.4'07124—dc21   99–006928

FIRST EDITION
HB Printing 10 9 8 7 6 5 4 3 2 1

The Jossey-Bass
Business & Management Series

To my husband, Don Werner,
who teaches me the difference
between nagging and coaching,
and who demonstrates that
even coaching has its limits.

To my parents, Madeline and Walter O'Neill,
who have shown me the value of bringing
both backbone and heart into the world.

Contents

· ·

Preface

· ·

I did not set out to become an executive coach. I evolved into one. As an internal consultant in a corporation, my results orientation and desire to be associated with successes made me aware that leaders were often inattentive to critical endeavors.

In my early years doing organization development work, I was also fortunate to have upper management bosses and clients that were willing to show me the business ropes while remaining open to my expertise in project management and facilitation. Therefore, I worked with these key decision makers on issues and undertakings about which they cared deeply.

Fortunately for my development, I often found myself in the executive office sitting across from a leader and talking about key issues. However, sometimes I was sitting with a leader who was disappointed with a project's progress. I had two choices: door number one—take personally what he was saying, that I and the rest of the executive team had let him down; or door number two—begin to notice a pattern in his behavior of leading that inevitably got us all to this point.[1] For my first year as an internal consultant, I chose door number one. Chalk it up to inexperience and a false sense of omnipotence (it must *always* be my fault). After a year, if I gave myself enough perspective, I noticed door number two opening quite frequently.

[1]Throughout the book I alternate "he" and "she," using them interchangeably as pronouns for the coach, the executive, and the employee.

Discovering a Passion for Coaching

So there I was, across from a disgruntled leader. I began to invite him into conversations about his frustrations, asking him what he thought the external causes were and what he may be contributing—though unintentionally—to the slowdown. These discussions were brief at first. As I became more skillful, I incorporated them into regular conversations I had with leaders regarding their business goals (Chapter Nine explores this transition to executive coaching in depth).

Another developmental thread in my coaching practice came from my work as a trainer in management development. Let me say right off that the classes I offered in leadership training were *good*. They were engaging, they were experiential, they were practical. However, the managers basically tolerated the training. They felt pretty smug and satisfied with their level of management skill "back on the floor"—until they got stuck. Then they would come to my office for help when they faced pressing and immediate dilemmas about high turnover, troublesome employees, low productivity, or a failed change effort. Their motivation to explore options for action increased dramatically over their interest about the same issues in my classes. When the managers came to me, I was quite willing to help them navigate through dilemmas about tasks or team challenges that they found personally daunting.

I was midstream in my own coaching practice before I thought of myself as an executive coach. It developed naturally out of organizational projects when leaders came to me for help. I was ten years into coaching when I began to articulate the coaching method that is in this book. Now, many years later, executive coaching is over half my work.

Coaching executives continues to be a passion for me because the work is challenging, inspiring, fun, and stimulating. I have been blessed with clients willing to look to themselves for the key ingredients necessary for significant change in their organizations. This kind of enterprise requires full engagement and risk taking on the part of both the leader and the coach.

What This Book Is About and Who It's For

The essence of coaching is helping leaders get unstuck from their dilemmas and assisting them in transferring their learning into results for the organization. *Executive Coaching with Backbone and Heart* addresses the complex pulls on the coach as she manages her own challenges in her work with executives.

The coaching field has gained broad interest from people in many disciplines. Some people come with a traditional business background and are coaching from one of the following organizational roles:

- internal organization development specialist

- external consultant

- human resources staff

- staff positions that require coaching skills; for example, project leads, engineers, information systems managers

Others are entering the field of executive coaching through different routes, such as counseling. Regardless of background, if you identify with one or more of the following statements, you will find this book useful:

- I have reached a plateau in my effectiveness as a coach and I need to find my way to the next level.

- I am not sure when one-on-one executive coaching should be expanded to working with the leader's team.

- My clients don't utilize me like they could.

- I have a "gut" feel for what works when I coach, but I don't know why it works. And sometimes it doesn't.

- The leader I am coaching resists my advice.

- How can I avoid becoming as anxious as my clients, so that I can continue to be useful to them?

- I want to increase my range of coaching within different venues: one-on-one, team, behind-the-scenes, live action.

- I want to improve the way I give tough feedback.

How This Book Is Different

Many books are available on coaching that describe the skills involved in coaching individuals to achieve both higher competence and greater motivation in their work. The audience for these books is managers learning how to be better coaches to their employees. Two excellent examples are Hargrove (1995) and Bell (1996). Though the writers focus on managers, business coaches in general can benefit from learning the building-block skills to coaching detailed in the literature. However, *Executive Coaching with Backbone and Heart* explores a different territory.

First, this book is written for those professionals who coach leaders of organizations. These executive coaches have the privilege of working with the men and women who lead and influence the direction of today's organizations. With this privilege comes a responsibility to partner with leaders in significant ways in order to contribute to successful change efforts. The work of executive coaches deserves its own literature in the field.

Second, unlike coaching methods that use techniques to leverage change in the client, *Executive Coaching with Backbone and Heart* focuses on the need for coaches to use their own *presence* with the client. Executive coaching is not about imposing skill training onto leaders. Fundamentally, it is about learning to *be* with leaders as they navigate through their world, finding key moments when they are most open to learning.

Let me be clear about being, learning, and doing. I do *not* mean that business outcomes should be ignored. There must be business results tied to coaching executives, and coaches should be business partners with leaders (Chapter Five). That can include helping develop necessary skills. **But the *key difference* in a change effort occurs when leaders face their own challenges in pulling off the business results and see how they get in their own way. In these pivotal moments, *how a coach manages herself* in the relationship to an executive facing those challenges can make the critical difference in the coaching outcome and therefore the business outcome.**

Third, this book focuses on the larger systems forces at play that require the attention of the executive coach. By *larger systems forces* I mean an organization's "force field" that shapes and influences the individuals working within it. Individuals respond to this field with their own emotional responses, thus either helping or hindering their effectiveness. Executives act and react within this field, along with everyone else they lead. If coaches fail to see how the system affects their clients, coaches will not understand why their interventions are sometimes ineffective. When coaches use skills presented in the general coaching literature and do not incorporate a systems approach, their actions will have limited results.

A systems viewpoint allows coaches to see the executive's world in a new way. *Executive Coaching with Backbone and Heart* explores a systems perspective and shows the implications and choices for the coach who attends to them.

Though coaches need a systems view to understand their client's system, they also need to know what effect their client's system has on *them*. This is the central premise and challenge of the book. **Coaches must tune in to how the client's force field impacts them, so they can maintain their equilibrium within it and help the leader to do the same.** When coaches hold this "bifocal" view—seeing their client in the system, and seeing themselves in the system—they can use the skill-building technologies in the coaching literature very effectively. In fact, the full power of these skills can finally be realized.

How This Book Is Organized

This book navigates between two cliffs: a *way of thinking* about coaching, and a *methodology* of coaching. I imagine this book as a river that runs through the canyon created by these two cliffs, needing both for its shape and power.

Just when it may seem as though a philosophy about presence and systems will lose its practical application, a method emerges to clarify the way. When the method becomes too rational for the topsy-turvy challenges of organizational life, a way of thinking about the use of the moment saves the method from trivialization. Perhaps the image is more like Alice through the looking glass when she finds herself in the wood of the vanishing path. When one is following a well-worn trail (the method), and that path disappears, one needs a way of attending to the forest (using one's presence in the moment) and orienting oneself within it.

Following is an overview and sequence of the content in the book.

Part One: Core Concepts—The Coach's Stance

Chapter One defines executive coaching and explores three core principles that underlie the book: coach self-management, a systems perspective, and a methodology compatible with the first two principles. The chapter explains the use of backbone and heart as it relates to the principle of coach self-management.

Chapter Two addresses the need to develop a signature presence, a way of bringing forward your backbone and heart as a coach. I describe four conditions that promote a strong presence, benefiting both coach and executive.

Chapters Three and Four cover specific, systemic dynamics in how to read an executive's system and how to recognize the system created between the executive and coach. There are many systems variables to study. Chapters Three and Four focus on some of the central ones. As a coach, you will find that when you attend to these systemic ideas, you are more likely to get at the core of what can unblock a leader and an organization from the corrosive qualities of their own system.

Part Two: Methodology—The Four Phases of Coaching

Chapters Five through Eight outline four essential phases to the coaching process: contracting, planning, live action intervening, and debriefing. These can help both beginning and experienced coaches provide a more in-depth service to their clients. The method, however, depends greatly upon bringing one's presence to coaching and using a systems lens. The combination of using systems thinking while bringing forward a signature presence creates a highly involving and effective process.

Part Three: Special Applications

Chapter Nine is for consultants and trainers, internal or external, who facilitate processes and projects in organizations. This chapter explores the times when leaders do not seek coaching directly. Chapter Nine indicates the kinds of conversations it is necessary to have with leaders before they start to see the consultant or trainer as a potential coach.

Chapter Ten covers how a coach can help an executive who needs to coach employees. Executive coaches often work with leaders who struggle with being effective coaches themselves. This chapter explains how to assist executives in becoming more effective coaches.

How to Use This Book

Executive Coaching with Backbone and Heart can be viewed as a workbook for coaches. Key ideas are in boldface throughout the text so that you can quickly note the areas most important to you. There are highlights of main ideas at the end of each chapter. You may look at the highlights first as an overview before diving into the chapter or scan them quickly for a review.

Appendix One contains the key skills of the coaching phases in a worksheet format. You can use it both to prepare for a coaching situation and as a self-assessment tool after a coaching session. Appendix Two covers key questions to ask clients during the various phases of the coaching method. Finally, Appendix Three explores the territory of combining coaching with consulting. It lists the competencies you need to have if you want to broaden your practice to include larger organizational consulting efforts.

There are stories from my coaching practice as well as typical vignettes placed throughout the book. They illustrate the coaching concepts and the method you can apply to the many challenging situations you may encounter when you coach leaders. I invite you to engage with the material in this book so that you can visit your past and future coaching experiences with new eyes.

Acknowledgments

· ·

I have increasing gratitude to those who contribute to my professional and personal journey. Their generous companionship creates a richly textured path for us to travel. It is with this appreciation that I thank the following people:

Dr. Judy Heinrich, Rob Schachter, and Roger Taylor: senior consultants at LIOS Consulting Corporation who practiced and developed this approach to executive coaching with me. In particular, I want to acknowledge the significant contribution that Rob Schachter has made to my perspective and practice while we worked as a consulting team to many diverse clients. His influence in this book is most directly felt in the coaching models of Chapter Four and our co-development of the Task 1, Task 2 approach in Chapter Ten.

Dr. Donald Williamson, Dr. Pamela Johnson, Dr. Timothy Weber, and Cheryl Cebula: faculty colleagues at the Leadership Institute of Seattle (LIOS)/Bastyr University who critiqued the book and offered perspectives from their disciplines and experience in organizational development and family systems.

Jack Fontaine, Dr. Ron Short, John Runyan, Christine Frissholz, Dale Scriven, Dr. Philip Heller, Diane Robbins, and Ellen Tichenor: colleagues who gave feedback that significantly influenced the direction of the book.

Byron Schneider, Julianna Gustafson, Margi Fox, and Janna Silverstein: Byron and Julianna, editors at Jossey-Bass, have been delightful. Their clarity of purpose gave the book added consistency while their gentleness urged me forward. Margi, a long-time friend and editor of my work, gave the guidance I needed to nudge the book to a final manuscript. Janna taught me to write a book proposal that publishers would read.

My clients and students: for their thirst for learning and willingness to risk new ways of seeing, being, and doing.

Barbara Guzzo, Libbie Stellas, Pat Lewis, Maureen Reid, Mary Hartrich, Judy Ryan, and Susie Leonard: godsisters giving many decades of support and friendship — they buoyed me during the writing process.

Don Werner, my husband: with love, he supported this effort, helped with initial graphics, and put up with having "the book" invade our home for longer than he ever imagined.

The Author

. . . .

Mary Beth O'Neill has worked in the field of organization consulting and leadership training, development, and coaching for over twenty years. She is currently a senior consultant at LIOS Consulting Corporation, a consulting organization of the Leadership Institute of Seattle (LIOS), college of applied behavioral science, at Bastyr University. O'Neill has coached a range of leaders: CEOs, senior vice presidents, plant managers, and first line supervisors. Her passion is in effectively linking people processes to business outcomes. Her current work in organizations encourages individual initiative and leadership from a systems perspective in order to achieve clearly defined business results.

O'Neill is a graduate faculty member in the master's program at LIOS/Bastyr University, which offers degrees with an emphasis either in corporate management and leadership, organization consultation and coaching, or systems counseling. She teaches courses in executive coaching, management of organizational change, change agent and consulting skills, action research, creation of business goals and measures, and systemic intervention in organizations.

Previously, she was the director of training and development at the Sheraton Seattle Hotel and Towers. She received the 1988 President's Award for her contributions toward productivity and quality at the Sheraton. O'Neill has a master's degree in applied behavioral science with an emphasis in organizational development from Whitworth College (1984). She also holds a master's degree in theology from Vanderbilt University (1977).

O'Neill has been the co-chair of Human Systems Development Professionals, an association of organizational development practitioners in the northwestern United States and Canada. She is a member of the Organization Development Network.

Executive Coaching with Backbone and Heart

Part I

. . . .

Core Concepts

The Coach's Stance

. . . .

An Introduction to Executive Coaching

COACH: What business challenges are you facing?

LEADER: We've got to get our division out of the cellar. Consistently, we have performed behind the other four divisions in the company. And the CEO's patience with us is wearing thin. I don't think he's going to put up with it much longer.

COACH: How much time have you got?

LEADER: On the outside, maybe twelve months.

COACH: What keeps you from getting the results that you want?

LEADER: My executive team isn't operating as a team. They're following their own business goals, not coordinating overlapping interests with other departments. In our meetings, when I ask for opinions on any issue, they don't respond if it's not in their functional area. We're not doing any creative problem solving.

COACH: What is challenging for you about this situation, given the disappointing results?

LEADER: I keep having to work two jobs—my own, and the vacancy on my team. In my first year as vice president, I've had three positions in a row open, and it's taken too long to fill each one. I'm trying to drive a car with one wheel constantly missing. Which doesn't give me much time to keep the larger view.

COACH: This sounds like a great setup for self-perpetuating burnout, both for you and for the members of your team. You'll never get the results you need to succeed if you don't carve out the space to lead your team.

LEADER: So tell me how to do it when I'm fighting fires!

COACH: You may be defaulting to managing what you know how to do, rather than doing what is needed. You may need to punch through your own edges in leading to get significantly different and higher results.

LEADER: Leading this effort is a big challenge for me. It's the first time I've managed multiple functions. I've never spent energy on managing as a discipline in itself. I get success through technical know-how. I could use some help in where to start.

COACH: Let's start with you defining more specifically what you expect from your team that would directly lead to higher results. Then we can look at what will be required of you to produce those results through your team.

Leaders hold a special position in the landscape of change. A leader's clarity of purpose, and his ability to connect the people in his organization to that purpose, go a long way toward mobilizing the necessary forces for change. There are times when executives need assistance to enact the responsibilities of their special position. Executive coaches can help because they know something about the change process.

What would you do if the leader from the vignette were referred to you for coaching? What would be your goal with him? What would you want to accomplish? How would you know you were being effective?

These are the questions that effective coaches ask themselves every time they start a new coaching relationship. They are also the questions that keep coaches—even good ones—up at night when the executive or the situation is at a particularly critical point.

When coaching conversations like this one are done well, over a period of time and with a motivated executive, they can lead to impressive results (as was the case for this leader, whose division became the top-producer in eight months).

This book explores what it takes to think and act in ways that are useful to executives. It will help you be a valuable resource to leaders when they need your resource the most.

What Is Executive Coaching?

The coaching partnership often begins when the leader is engaged in a dilemma and feels stymied. As mentioned in the Preface, the essence of executive coaching is helping leaders get unstuck from their dilemmas and assisting them to transfer their learning into results for the organization.

Coaches bring the kind of trained yet natural curiosity of a journalist or an anthropologist to the leader's work situation. In addition, coaches typically

- Share conceptual frameworks, images, and metaphors with executives.

- Encourage rigor in the way leaders organize their thinking, visioning, planning, and expectations.

- Challenge executives to their own competence or learning edge.

- Build leaders' capacity to manage their own anxiety in tough situations.

By *executive* I mean leaders who are in the top and upper levels of their organizations—the CEOs, vice presidents, plant managers, and executive directors of organizations. I define the executive's job in three broad areas:

1. **Communicating the territory,** that is, the purpose, the vision, and goals of the organization to key constituencies, and outlining opportunities and challenges.

2. **Building relationships and facilitating interactions** that result in outstanding team performance.

3. **Producing results and outcomes,** more from the direct efforts of others than from his own efforts.

Executive coaching is the process of increasing the leader's skill and effectiveness in accomplishing these three responsibilities of leadership. These areas can be used as a kind of checklist for the coach to make a quick assessment of the leader's ability and degree of attention he gives to each one. For example, in the opening story, the leader was clear about the third responsibility, the results. He even had a sense about what was missing in the second area, the interactions he needed from his team. But he had yet to act on that knowledge—he was not defining the expectations he had for his team's behavior. Neither was he communicating to his team, with any conviction, the territory ahead, that is, his vision.

Some of you coach one-on-one with leaders exclusively. Others, myself included, use coaching as one tool of many in larger organizational change projects with leaders (see Appendix Three). Even though I coach within a larger change effort, *Executive Coaching with Backbone and Heart* focuses on the one-on-one, executive–coach work relationship. Why? Because it is so critical.

There can be a false assumption that this relationship happens in isolation from the dynamics of the executive's team. It does not, even when you only coach the leader. Whether coaching the executive happens with the team or away from them, the coaching relationship is set within the *context* of the team and the organization. One of the purposes of executive coaching is to turn the leader toward her team. This approach can enhance both the team's and the leader's participation and contribution.

I do want to acknowledge the special concerns executives have who are at the very top of their organizations. Top executives deal with issues of stockholder or partner ownership, succession, loyalty, strategic alliances, and positioning in the marketplace. They also suffer from a belief that they should not ask for help, which exacerbates their "lonely at the top" experience. Coaches of top executives need to treat these matters with seriousness and without being intimidated by the issues themselves.

The biggest difference I find in coaching top executives as opposed to middle executives is one of tone and pace. Top executives seem to require more toughness from those who partner with them. By toughness I mean bringing less tact, with a faster route to the punch line—in other words, more directness, sooner. Even though the pace is quicker and the tone more blunt with top executives, the coaching approach of this book works with middle executives as well as the top leaders in organizations.

Four Essential Ingredients of Executive Coaching

Let's go back again and follow along with the coach-executive conversation at the beginning of this chapter. The coach's sequencing of questions carries four essential ingredients of executive coaching. The first is having a **results orientation to a leader's problem** (*"What business challenges are you facing? How much time have you got?"*). To lose sight of outcomes is to waste the time, money, and energy of the leader. The organization needs him to stay focused on what will produce the key goods, services, or information that define that organization's success. A coach's job is to have a mission paralleling the leader's drive for results.

The second ingredient is **partnership.** The coach becomes a partner in the executive's journey toward greater competence and effectiveness. Through the general flow of the conversation (and in the question, *"What keeps you from getting the results you want?"*), the coach begins to stand shoulder to shoulder with the executive in untangling and laying out the many factors, forces, and dilemmas facing the leader. Within this collegiality, the coach inquires, stimulates, and challenges the leader to perform at his optimal level.

The third ingredient is the ability **to engage the executive in the specific leadership challenges he faces** (*"What is challenging for you about this situation, given the disappointing results?"*). This helps him explore what pulls him off course and what he typically avoids. He might also see the wake he creates in others as he works through his agenda. This is often a difficult focus. Leaders naturally resist concentrating on their own actions while they look externally to others for results. Within their partnership the coach confronts the executive to look at ways he may be his own worst enemy in the problem situation.

In the fourth ingredient, the coach **links team behaviors to the bottom-line goals, and points out the need for executives to set specific expectations of their teams** to achieve the results. (*"Let's start with you defining more specifically what you expect from your team that would directly lead to higher results."*) This is an essential connection, defining as much as possible what specific people processes are most relevant to these distinct business goals. It keeps leaders focused on their results orientation but now widens their view to what they most need from their teams to get there. It is important in this conversation (linking results with team behaviors) to keep the leader's responsibility central (the coach's last comment in the dialogue: *"Then we can look at what will be required of you to produce those results through your team."*) This cycles back to the third ingredient, exploring the leader's challenges to do what is required.

Core Principles That Guide Executive Coaching

When I coach executives, I hold three core values or principles that guide my approach. They provide the main framework for executive coaching. These principles provide an awareness that allows for an exponential increase in coaching effectiveness. The first two principles—bringing your signature presence to the coaching process, and using a systems perspective in your coaching practice—are discussed extensively in the Core Concepts section of Part One in the book. The third principle—applying a coaching method—is fleshed out in the methodology chapters of Part Two.

. . . .

PRINCIPLE NUMBER 1: *Bringing your own signature presence to coaching is the major tool of intervention.*

Everyone calls on leaders to bring who they are and the best of themselves to their roles. They are challenged to lead authentically and to utilize a more integrated self. It would be hypocritical for us in our role as coaches to encourage leaders to do this and not bring ourselves forward as well.

Bringing your self—your own unique, signature presence—means that you inhabit the role of coach in ways that no one else does. And you do not perform techniques *on* executives. Leaders can pick up a cookie-cutter technique instantly. Instead, leaders need true partners in their developmental process. I have already used the word *partner* several times. It is a deep value that I hold in working with leaders. They require peers who will meet them in their most daunting work challenges. They deserve coaches who are willing to be who they are and not hide behind a role.

The coaching relationship is built on trust, the ability mutually to give and receive feedback, the ability to be *present*—on the part of both the coach and the leader—to learn from their experiences. It is a highly interactive process. As a coach, bringing your signature presence can evoke the signature presence of leaders, helping them to see that bringing themselves to their goals, challenges, and relationships is one of the central requirements for their success.

. . . .

PRINCIPLE NUMBER 2: *Using a systems perspective keeps you focused on fundamental processes. These forces either promote or impede the interactions and results of the executives you coach.*

A systems perspective is highly relevant to executive coaches. When you focus too narrowly on your client alone (the smallest sphere)—her personal challenges, the goals she has for herself, and the inner obstacles that keep her from being successful—you miss the whole grand "ecosystem" in which she functions. She is both influencing and being influenced by an entire web of interrelationships in and around the organization—the team, other departments, vendors, and customers (the midsize sphere). Also important are external contexts, which include the global economy and the natural environment (the largest sphere). It is essential to pay attention to the system, the nested set of spheres, where your client works (Figure 1.1). Those forces may have an enormous effect on your client's success. They influence the very challenges, goals, and obstacles she faces, the ones you are working on together. This is a nonlinear perspective that allows you as a coach to recognize patterns of interaction within and across spheres.

Viewing an organization systemically constitutes the foundation of Peter Senge's work (1990). He emphasizes the effects of feedback loops on a system. Feedback loops are the consequences or repercussions of a system's behavior that interact with other contexts and then provide input back into the system, acting as either a brake or an accelerator to people's activity. He focuses on the way slight changes can alter the entire system.

The perspective I use here is compatible with Senge and uses the mindset of feedback loops. But the scope is different. Rather than looking at how the external environment interacts between the largest sphere and the organization, I look at the system of a leader and the individuals and groups in the midsize sphere around her.

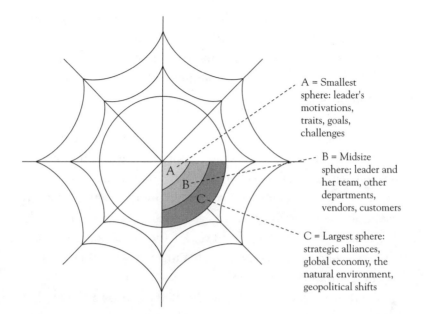

A = Smallest sphere: leader's motivations, traits, goals, challenges

B = Midsize sphere; leader and her team, other departments, vendors, customers

C = Largest sphere: strategic alliances, global economy, the natural environment, geopolitical shifts

Figure 1.1. The Leader's System.[1]

Why keep my view on the midsize sphere rather than the largest one? Leaders reflexively look out to the horizon. They constantly scan for large themes, trends, threats, and opportunities. In fact, leaders can learn to do this better by being introduced to systems thinking through the largest sphere, as Senge and others have done.

What has been underdeveloped, however, is the systems focus on the midsize sphere. Leaders' problems can come from their own backyard—the system of interaction in place between them and the people they work with most closely. If we as coaches can help them see the midsize system and the part they play, we help them change their way of interacting. Executives can then unlock an enormous amount of their own and others' resources to learn from and work with the larger environment (the largest sphere).

·   ·   ·   ·   ·   ·   ·

PRINCIPLE NUMBER 3: *Applying a coaching method is power-fully effective when you also use the first two principles, bringing your signature presence and using a systems approach. Otherwise, the method will achieve only short-term results.*

The coaching method I outline in this book follows four straightforward stages: contracting, planning, live action interven-ing, and debriefing. Those of you who are professionals in the orga-nizational development field will recognize the methodology as classic action research applied to coaching. Like action research, this coaching method drives toward achieving a business result while building the capacity of clients to apply what they learn to other organizational situations.

There is a value embedded in the method. It is the belief that leaders have within them most of the resources they need to address the very issues that seem most daunting. This does not refer to an isolationist self-sufficiency. Leaders are certainly interdepen-dent with those around them. I am referring to the resilience indi-viduals have to mobilize the resources at hand, both in them and in the people around them, to address pressing organizational challenges.

The four phases of the methodology have a linear, step-by-step progression. However, nonlinear human responses can undo the most sublimely constructed methodologies. Coaching methods can unravel in our hands at the very times we depend on them most: with executives on the verge of implementing a vision, leaders in the midst of large change efforts, or executives in the heat of inter-departmental conflicts. As an antidote to these times of chaos and stress, I advocate mining the resources of one's presence, focusing on what happens in and among the human beings caught in the dilemma. Making the most of the moment can be *the* leverage point for change when it is explored fully and then linked back to a method with a results orientation.

The more you increase your coaching ability to practice from these three principles, the more successful you will be in evoking, promoting, and challenging the leader to do the same. Executives can use the three principles as well. They need to find **their signature presence** in the unique way that they lead. A **systems perspective** can keep them from getting lost in the patterns and processes of the organization. Their **method** of leading needs to be informed by the ability to mine the moment.

Coaching with Backbone and Heart

In bringing your signature presence, you bring your ideas, biases, and challenging suggestions to your clients. You *also* need to maintain strong relationships and connections with those same leaders. **Backbone is about saying what your position is, whether it is popular or not. Heart is staying in relationship and reaching out even when that relationship is in conflict.**

These two functions work together and interrelate. Each does not do well in isolation from the other. Neither way is effective in business situations when it is polarized from the other function: for example, speaking strongly while shutting others down or being highly empathetic while others do not know what you think. Executive coaching is a continual dance of balancing backbone and heart while you work with the leader.

One way to test for your own ability to do each one is to take an inventory of your coaching interactions:

Bringing Backbone

- Does my client know what I think? How often do I say, "I agree with you," or "I disagree with you" and clearly state why?

- Do I say what I need from the executive in our working relationship in order to be most effective with her?

- Can I give my position without blame or becoming defensive?

- Can I state my opinion without jargon or fancy concepts?

- Can I give hard feedback when I need to?

Bringing Heart

- Do I understand my client's situation?

- Can I clearly articulate his position and reflect it back to him?

- Do I identify and tell the leader the hunches I have about possible deeper reactions, feelings, and thoughts he is leaving unsaid?

- When there is a disagreement or conflict between the leader and me, do I keep engaging with him or do I retreat and disengage?

- Do I continue to stay in touch?

- Do I express appreciation for the degree of difficulty a situation may be for a leader and also the degree of accomplishment he has achieved?

Everyone seems to come equipped with the ability to show either backbone or heart more naturally than the other characteristic. Executive coaching requires you to do both, whether they come naturally or not. Executives deserve nothing less from you. As an executive coach, you need to ensure that you develop your competence to access and enact both functions in your work with leaders.

Likewise, a coach tracks an executive's ability to show both backbone and heart. When it comes to pulling off the tasks of leadership, it is a rare leader who is a natural in both areas.

Executives bring backbone by standing up for and articulating their positions in the face of others challenging them. They bring heart when they have compassion for those they lead, seeking to understand their challenges, concerns, and ideas. In other words, leaders have the ability to tune in to where others are. The more you learn how to live a balance of backbone and heart in your coaching work, the more you will know how to help leaders to do the same. The upcoming chapters in this book address some ways to do just that.

* * * * * * *

CHAPTER ONE HIGHLIGHTS

What Is Executive Coaching?

1. Coaching activities

   - Use your curiosity to learn about the leader's situation
   - Share conceptual frameworks
   - Invite the client to be more rigorous in his thinking
   - Build the leader's capacity to manage his anxiety

2. Assess the executive's ability to

   - Communicate the territory
   - Build relationships and facilitate interactions
   - Produce results and outcomes

Four Essential Ingredients of Executive Coaching

1. Bring a results orientation to the leader's problem.

2. Be a partner.

3. Engage the executive in her specific leadership challenges.

4. Link team behaviors to bottom-line goals.

Core Principles That Guide Executive Coaching

1. Bring your own signature presence.

2. Use a systems perspective.

3. Apply the coaching method within the context of a signature presence and a systems viewpoint.

Coaching with Backbone and Heart

- Backbone—state your positions clearly.
- Heart—tune in to the relationship with understanding and compassion.

• • • • • • •

2

. . . .

Developing a Strong Signature Presence

Why is signature presence so critical for coaches? Dealing with organizational change and dilemmas is not for the faint-hearted. The business arena contains risks, opportunities, dangers, and dead-ends: All can make a leader flinch.

Coaches are colleagues to leaders at exactly those times when they may flinch—or fight back, or dig in, or any number of responses. Coaches show up in the executive's office when the leader is most likely to act from an automatic, less-effective response. A coach has to bring her own presence in order to be a contributing partner. Otherwise, the leader's interactional force field of dilemmas can also pull in the coach (*interactional fields* receive thorough coverage in Chapter Three). When the coach succumbs to the same dilemmas as the leader, she does not help but contributes to the problem instead.

The Central Tool

Presence means bringing your self when you coach—your values, passion, creativity, emotion, and discerning judgment—to any given moment with a client. You bring your resourcefulness and authenticity to your work. You develop skills in two arenas: the courage to speak and command attention and, when needed, the ability to become an invisible part of the background.[1]

Presence means developing and **increasing your tolerance** for a host of situations many people actively avoid: ambiguity, daunting challenge, others' anxiety or disapproval, and your own stress. Presence stands in the midst of any of these reactions, does not shut them out, and acts anyway. In the face of internal or external resistance, you refuse to back away from the moment at hand. *Signature* presence is moving through these moments in a way unique to you, thus making the most of your own strengths, interests, and eccentricities.

If you do not develop yourself enough to withstand a leader's stress, you default to actions that handle your own discomfort but are not useful to her. The worst case scenario occurs when you do not even know you are in this state, and you run your client through a methodology that rings hollow to the dilemma the leader faces.

When you realize that you have absorbed the anxiety and feelings of responsibility from your client, there is a glimmer of hope. When you can say to yourself, "Oops, I'm stuck. I'm as anxious and nonresourceful as she is," you begin your way back to equilibrium. Questions to ask at these times are

- Why am I doing what I'm doing?

- Is this truly good for the client?

- Am I doing this to lower my own stress, even as I imagine that I act in the clients' best interest?

The more you maintain your presence, the more you assist the leader. You can clearly get at the core of the issues. You successfully challenge the leader and offer genuine support. Presence is easy when you are not anxious, but it is illusive when you are. The problem is how to get back to your presence when you have lost it.

Self-Differentiation

You strengthen the ability to regain your presence in anxious moments through a process called **self-differentiation.**[2] It creates a balance between two major tasks in relationships—in this case, working relationships. One capability is to clearly articulate where you stand with a judgment, a decision, or a bottom line (**backbone** work). *At the same time,* you endeavor to stay connected and tuned in to those with whom you take the stand or decision (the work of the **heart**). An image I find useful for self-differentiation is that of a gyroscope. It constantly tilts, moves, and rolls with outside forces, yet the inner mechanism stays level, no matter how topsy-turvy the whole system becomes. **Interactional equilibrium** is the ability to maintain yourself and your relationships while pulled by the forces of fear, conflict, and anxiety.

The absence of self-differentiation causes a state of **reactivity.** Essentially this stance refers to the times when we lose our balance internally and respond in an automatic, ineffective way. Reactivity shows many faces as backbone and heart fall out of balance. We can alienate others, or maintain a too timid posture. You may cave in on a position, or become overly rigid and closed to influence. You might cut off the relationship and distance from others or pay too much attention to other people's moods by smoothing over rough spots.

No one achieves self-differentiation 100 percent of the time— actually, not even 70 or 80 percent. To accomplish this balance a simple majority of the time is a real feat. Most of us constantly fall into reactivity, then pull out of it and face the next challenge. **The goal is to decrease the amount of time we are reactive and to recover equilibrium more quickly.** With practice you *see opportunities* to take stands while staying connected and then *enact them.* The more you as coach recover from your reactivity with less damage to yourself and your relationships, the more valuable you are to those with whom you work. Examples of actions you could take as a coach that maintain the balance of backbone and heart include the following:

1. Disagree with a specific   AND   1. Continue to understand
process the leader is using   and support the leader's
                                                         larger goals

2. Give your best thinking   AND   2. Refuse to sell a specific
on an issue, not holding   action plan to an
back your own biases   executive, knowing the
                                        leader needs to have
                                        ownership for his
                                        own plan

3. Challenge the leader's   AND   3. Offer him help to
commitment to a planned   become more consistent
course because of his
inconsistent actions, and
be clear that you will end
the contract if the
inconsistency continues

Any coach who brings this kind of balance to her work would
be in high demand. The effective coach is not intimidated by the
leader and does not join the executive's viewpoint too quickly.
However, the coach is able to grasp the leader's stance and convey
understanding and compassion for the leader's dilemmas. In other
words, the coach has the ability to be an independent thinker while
working interdependently with the client.

*So how can I pull off both backbone and heart work? Is there a way to
strengthen my presence? Are there ways to get back to the balance?*

Strengthen Your Presence

A set of critical actions contributes to your ability as coach to regain
your presence in the moment and do so with creativity. The following four approaches promote a healthy resilience in you as you
work with your client:

- **Identify and sustain a goal for yourself in each
coaching session.**

- **Manage yourself in the midst of ambiguity.**

- Increase your tolerance for the reactivity within you and in others around you.

- Bring immediacy to the moment.

These approaches are not techniques. It would be foolish to assume one could attain them merely through insight and understanding. They require a willingness to enter into a maturing process that builds resiliency. The more a person engages in the lifelong work of honing these actions, the more a strong sense of presence can emerge. The stronger your presence, the easier it is to access these approaches. Mastering them is a lifelong process.[3] All four approaches appear continually in the coaching method outlined in Chapters Five through Eight.

Identify and Sustain Your Goal

In some ways, this approach sets the stage for all the others. There is no place to go without a goal. And when a coach becomes reactive, it is harder to hold onto that goal, even to remember it. When I say goal, I mean choosing a goal for yourself to accomplish when you are in a coaching session with an executive. *What, have a goal for myself? Shouldn't I be helping the leader with his goal?* The clearer you are about what you want to accomplish in the session while you work on the leader's agenda, the more of a resource you are to your client. You can take the following steps to identify and sustain your goal:

1. Choose a content and/or process goal.
2. Know your vulnerability in a reactive system.
3. Remember your goal.
4. Be more committed to your goal than easing your discomfort in the moment.

A goal can be about **content**—*what* is to be accomplished in the coaching session. Or a goal can be about **process**—*how* a coach wants to be in the session. A **content goal** could include any of the following:

- Get the commitment of the leader to a coaching contract.

- Help the executive establish outcome measures for his change initiative.

- Prioritize with the leader the list of issues he needs to address.

The goals below demonstrate a focus on **process**:

- Show understanding for the executive's world and challenges.

- Stay on track in the session, even if the leader shows impatience.

- Give the tough feedback that until now you have been withholding.

It is one thing to establish a goal and another thing entirely to *sustain* a goal. **You must become familiar with your own points of vulnerability within a reactive system.** By vulnerability I mean the **triggers** that can occasion your knee-jerk, unthinking response and cause you to let go of your goal in the session. Triggers differ for each person, but the following list contains some common ones:

- Being challenged by a dominating person.

- Facing high rates of change.

- Receiving requests for help by a highly dependent person.

• Having a client who rushes from one activity to the
  next, including the coaching sessions

Reconnecting with your goal when you become reactive goes
a long way to lessen the effects of your anxiety. First, **realize that
you *will* go on automatic when your stress is high.** Adrenaline
responses easily take over. Once you acknowledge this without
berating yourself, you can get back on track. Here are some clues
that you have let go of your goal: Either your spine dissolves into
jelly or you become as rigid as a stone wall; either you completely
lose empathy for your client or you begin to see the world only
through your client's eyes. These extreme responses provide a sure
sign of reactivity.

After you realize you went on automatic, then **remember your
goal** in the heat of the moment. *(What was it I said I wanted to
accomplish in this session? Oh yeah!)* Once you recall it, **be more committed to your goal than fighting or fleeing from the intense discomfort you feel in the moment—and act on that commitment.**
To the extent that you thoughtfully identified an appropriate goal
before the session, you can still trust that goal when you temporarily lose sight of it. Grabbing hold of it and proceeding provides the
anchor that calms your boat in stormy seas.

Here is an example of what identifying and sustaining a goal can
look like.

✦ ✦ ✦ ✦ ✦ ✦ ✦

Luke

Luke was in a tough position, and I was in a tough position with
Luke. His boss, the president, "suggested" that he develop his staff
into a stronger team in order to operate more efficiently. Luke

---

Note: Names and identifying details have been changed to protect the privacy of
individuals and organizations.

would not have chosen to initiate this work. He responded to the president's suggestion because he felt pressured to do it.

After spending some time with Luke and his staff, three things became clear: (1) the staff was not sure about the purpose of the development and whether the president truly backed it, (2) Luke needed to have a frank conversation with his boss about issues that festered between them—these issues affected the boss's support of the department's work, and (3) Luke needed extensive development of himself as a leader for this team to take any significant step forward.

My anxiety increased because I sensed Luke's passivity in this endeavor; he was mainly going through the paces. To move ahead without a higher investment on his part would accomplish nothing and waste money on the effort. Worse, it would actually damage the morale of the department if they experienced one more false start in a long line of previous half-baked change efforts. My track record of coaching for and facilitating successful change efforts was on the line as well.

I established three goals for myself as I went into a critical meeting with Luke: (1) proceed only if he commits to working on his relationship to his boss as it relates to the department (content goal), (2) proceed only if he commits to developing himself as a leader (content goal), and (3) while working on the first two goals, offer support as well as challenge to Luke during this meeting (process goal).

Luke started the meeting with his usual passive affability. As I talked about my thinking and concerns regarding what was needed, his demeanor changed dramatically. Luke grew silent, then became argumentative. He said, "I don't understand what this project has to do with my relationship to my boss! Why are you making it so difficult to proceed?" We came to an impasse. He was unwilling to commit to the two bottom lines I had established, and I was unwilling to move ahead without them. I was within five minutes of ending the contract.

As for my third goal (challenge and support), my bottom lines were extremely challenging to Luke. For a long time, he avoided dealing with the expectations and judgments of his boss. But I continued to highlight the need for it in this project.

I said, "Luke, I don't think a boss has to be involved in every team development project. But on this one, it is critical—even a make or break issue. Part of the team development work is to clarify the goals for the department. You are telegraphing to your team deeply mixed messages about what you expect of them. And that's not just because you are unclear. It is because your boss is giving *you* mixed messages. It's time to clear them up with him. Otherwise, you waste this team's time and we might as well call it off."

Throughout the meeting I also continuously offered Luke support for his efforts to work on his relationship to his boss, should he choose to move in that direction. I let him know that because this step would be so challenging for him, the majority of our coaching work would be around it—I was there to help him if he wanted it.

Though he resisted the issue for a long time, Luke understood the stakes were too high for him to do nothing. He found a way to frame what kind of clarification work he would do with his boss to get the project under way. I decided it was enough of a commitment. We could proceed with the team project.

• • • • • • •

These issues continued to be part of the fabric of my work with Luke. This was no "magic bullet" conversation. However, we had more effective sessions because I went after my goals from the beginning of my work with Luke. Sustaining your own goals as a coach in your sessions with the executive gives you more focus, particularly in times of ambiguity.

Manage Yourself Amid Ambiguity

By *ambiguity* I mean the business situations that are by nature unclear and murky. The loss of clarity doesn't result from anyone's lack of intelligence or problem-solving capability. The factors never by themselves become transparent. Many leaders try to suppress ambiguity, rather than acknowledge it, even to themselves. Others give up in the face of it, believing choosing a next step to be too treacherous. During times of ambiguity, people fill in gaps of information with rumor, fears, assumptions, and paranoia.

In the midst of ambiguity, coaches can also lose their bearings. This is a humbling experience. The root word of *humble* is "humus"—ground, compost, soil. When you are reactive, you are not grounded. To reground yourself, you need to take the lay of the land and see your circumstances for what they are rather than what you wish them to be.

How you **manage yourself in ambiguity** is the key. Here are five actions you can take—and suggest your client take—in these situations:

1. **Acknowledge the ambiguity.**

2. **Distinguish for yourself where you are clear and where you are unclear about the situation.**

3. **Articulate to others the boundary of your clarity and your lack of clarity.**

4. **Say what it is you want to do, given the situation.**

5. **Tell others what you need from them.**

With this approach, you can cultivate a kind of decisiveness even in the midst of confusion. It is refreshing to acknowledge both your clarity and your ambiguity, rather than hide it or become victimized by it. You can be clear about what you know and what you do not know. This allows others to come forward with the same, seeing the conversation as a contribution rather than an acknowledgment of their inadequacy. Then you can fill in the *perceived* gaps with real information and discover the actual gaps. Building on this kind of dialogue, you articulate what you want to do, and what you need from others, moving the discussion from free-floating anxiety, to collecting information, to taking action.

Obviously, leaders need to learn how to manage themselves in the middle of ambiguity. *But how is it useful for coaches? Isn't any lack of clarity in the coach detrimental for the leader?* It can actually be a good example for leaders to experience a coach acknowledging areas where she encounters the deep ambiguity of the leader's situation. In the following story, I used the various steps of managing myself in ambiguity. You may notice they do not necessarily follow a sequential order. Managing ambiguity is not a linear exercise.

· · · · · · ·

Bill

Bill was the leader of two departments that had recently merged. On top of that, the organization had a new CEO who indicated that the company would be reorganizing sometime next year. Bill had formidable tasks at hand. He had to coordinate new job expectations within the consolidated department, maintain the same level of productivity that the company needed from them, and respond quickly to any upcoming reorganization even though there was no established structure or start date for it. The situation was by nature deeply ambiguous.

Bill wanted help in figuring out how to organize his own people so they could function in the midst of all this uncertainty. The first step Bill identified was the easiest. Since he wanted to get the two departments working as one, he decided he would not figure this out on his own, or leave it up to the half of the department who historically took on problem-solving. Instead, he engaged the best thinking of the people in the whole department.

Bill invited me to join him and his team on a retreat where they addressed these issues. My role was to coach him during the meeting while they designed a process they could use to lead them to more clarity.

The retreat started off well enough but hit an inevitable snag when no one saw a way through all the unknown factors facing them. The "no one" included me. I did not see a way to proceed either. I berated myself for not seeing a clear way out—I was the coach, after all! Bill and the team were all looking at me expectantly. I started to scan—what was going on? (*2. Distinguish for yourself where you are clear and where you are unclear about the situation.*)

· · · · · · ·

The ambiguity of their situation did not result from a flaw in the design of the retreat—the right people were in the room; they had all the information that was available from the CEO; they were looking at current realities, future opportunities, and obstacles; they held discussions in matrixed groups; and they were a highly creative group of people. The ambiguity debilitating their progress occurred because there *was no clear way through it.* I have come to appreciate what they experienced much more now than I did then: a chaos preceding the emergence of a new way of thinking. They were in the position to discover a new way to organize. They could not see it because this new way did not exist apart from moving through the ambiguity.[4]

· · · · · · ·

Bill, continued

All of them, as well as myself, had hit a patch of deep fog. (*1. Acknowledge the ambiguity.*) I told Bill in the presence of his team that it was time to name "what is clear and unclear, and what do we need?" I also said that it felt uncomfortable, not because they were doing anything wrong, but because the situation was by nature unclear. It could also mean that they were on the verge of a burst of creativity because original thinking starts when they are willing to stop hanging on to the familiar territory and start moving out into the unknown. I told Bill to hang out in the confusion and hold less tightly to their need to have clarity quickly. (*4. Say what it is you want.*)

If this had been a pep talk I would have failed miserably because my saying this did not automatically give Bill the relief of a clear path. The team continued to struggle with the issues. After a while, however, one of the team leaders thought of a way to arrange the department into groups so that they reenergized their creative thinking around the issues. They figured out how to lightly organize themselves—identifying a fluid matrix—so that they could work on current demands from the rest of the organization and also identify internal areas that were most susceptible to reorganization.

I shared with Bill and his team what I knew. No matter how they organized themselves now or identified the issues for restructuring, they needed to find a way to clarify decision-making authority and task responsibility (3. *Articulate to others the boundary of your clarity and your lack of clarity*). Otherwise their "quick response" mechanisms would be undone at the time they needed them the most and they would waste the benefit of their preplanning. Bill then saw his responsibility to ensure such decision-making clarity. The teams also realized they needed to insist that Bill be clear with them about what authority they had for which specific issues. (5. *Tell others what you need from them.*)

• • • • • • •

I admired their development of a fluid structure that serviced and anticipated changes. And I was glad that we all had continued to manage the ambiguity by staying in conversation, distinguishing what is known and not known, clarifying plans to move ahead, and stating the needs that people had of others.

Increase Your Tolerance for Reactivity

In some ways, this is the essence of presence, having tolerance for others' anxiety and reactivity, and for their disappointment or disapproval. In addition, you have to deal with your own anxiety with external or internal resistance to come forward in the moment. We all have our own tolerance levels for uncomfortable situations. We have our individual responses—fight, flight, save the day, placate—the list is endless. These responses get in the way of helping a client or a system regain maximum functioning. They act more like a circuit breaker to our own fuse box—automatic responses to an overload of input that shortcircuits our own system.

When I am uncomfortable in a situation, I sometimes feel helpless and inadequate. I ask myself, "What good am I doing at this point?" My feeling of helplessness can draw out responses in me that, looking back on them, seem inappropriate and ineffective in the situation. I turn to the first thing I can think of just to find resolution as soon as possible. It is not the leader I am fleeing, but the discomfort I feel. The best thing I can do for my client is to increase my level of tolerance for my anxiety so that I can truly be with her, instead of being distracted by my own reactivity.

Increasing your tolerance is by nature an unbearable experience, because the pull of the old reaction is so strong. However, you can take steps to help yourself get to the other side:

1. **Identify the trigger to your reactivity.**

2. **Figure out your typical reaction to that trigger.**

3. **Choose an alternative response to get you started down a different path.**

4. **Stay on track with the goal you have for yourself in the session.**

Actually, naming these steps can be deceiving. These are necessary actions, but taking them may not be sufficient to increase your tolerance for reactivity. You also have to be willing to enter a void before getting to the other side. Increasing your tolerance means strengthening an emotional muscle that can hold on in that void. It's more than doing any specific action.

This growth comes with exposure to the situations themselves, just as an emergency room physician's comfort with trauma is higher than that of a medical student's. An enhanced skill level due to education and practice with the methodology helps. Using the above steps expands your ability to cope with the anxiety. Another avenue is exploring new ways to react to stress other than those you learned early in the first "organization" you participated in—your family.[5] Whatever it takes—and it takes all of the above—your job is to strengthen that muscle so you can remain present with your clients.

Though they do not offer a perfect solution, the steps can provide an important tool. Once you are ready to increase your tolerance, you need to **identify the trigger** for your reactivity in specific situations. Your particular trigger can be anything. Is it your client's tone of voice? Is it a particular subject matter? Does it involve a question of your ability? The content and the context of the triggers are unique to you.

Once you understand what causes your reaction, you **learn to identify your reaction to the trigger.** Reactivity is a response that happens automatically without thinking about it. You may be well into your reaction before you notice it. What are typical reactive responses on your part? Do you feel guilty and skulk away? Do you get angry and lash out? Do you feel defensive and explain your position? Get to know your habitual responses.

Choosing an alternative response gives you time to think, ahead of the action, about what you want to do instead. You will rarely be able to plan in the heat of an automatic response, so knowing your own habits is critical. You can see them in the moment (*"There I go again"*) and have something in mind to break the trance. As an example of planned responses, you could pause and give yourself time to think. Or plan to ask about the position and concerns of the other person. Or remember to keep working toward your goal.

Staying on track with your goal is the central point of developing yourself as a less reactive person. As I said earlier, reactivity leads you away from your goal. However, your goal can calm you in the midst of your reactivity. There has to be something worth all the discomfort of dealing with automatic responses, your own and others. It's to accomplish something! This is why <u>choosing a worthy goal is a necessary condition of presence.</u>

An example of increasing tolerance for others' and one's own reactivity happened to me with a leader with whom I had a long, collaborative working relationship.

* * * * * *

Annette

Periodically, Annette would ask me to do a particular task. I was able to do it, but it was inappropriate to my contract with her. She wanted me to oversee a committee on human resource standards with her staff. There were people in the organization who were much more appropriate for the role. If I chaired the committee, it would undermine the skill development of others who reported to her. Annette did not see it that way. She knew I was a good facilitator, and she just wanted the job done.

Because everything else in our contract worked well, it was personally difficult for me to refuse her request. Yet I was very sure that saying no was the best response for the organization and ultimately for her. On the occasions I agreed to an activity outside the bounds of my role, I always regretted it. I saw that I contributed to a continued weakness in her staff and resented my own compromise. Whenever I found myself in Annette's office in the middle of this conversation, I could feel the internal pull to say yes. My anxiety went up as I imagined the degree of disappointment she would have in me if I refused.

Finally, I understood my discomfort. I found it hard to sit in the midst of her disappointment and irritation. Period. I had about a five-minute endurance for it before I backed down. When I realized this, I resolved to hold my ground no matter how long it took (if I could just get to the sixth minute!). One way I thought I could endure her reaction was by being prepared to say, over and over again, "I know you find it disappointing, but I am not able to do it."

In our next meeting, for fifteen minutes Annette cajoled, flattered, threatened, and bargained with me. For fifteen minutes I repeated my mantra, "I know you find it disappointing . . . ." It seemed as though it went on much longer. That's being in the void—totally out of a comfort zone and continuing to hang on anyway. She finally stopped. And she never asked me to take on the task again. One of her managers did it instead, and it helped him develop further in his job.

· · · · · · ·

Increasing tolerance for moments of reactivity can allow you to hang on long enough to experience something new, instead of the same old action-reaction-counterreaction. Hanging on longer may mean for twenty seconds, two hours, or two months. It is increasing the strength and stamina of your "tolerance muscle." You experience yourself as an adventurer in a land few travel—enduring reactivity long enough for the new moment to occur. It does not arrive when everyone follows old responses.

The process is sometimes like standing on a windy hill in a hailstorm—bracing, but daunting. However, even an incremental increase in tolerance can provide a geometric gain in bringing newness to a situation—either a dramatically different resistance, or a breakthrough with the client, or both.

Bring Immediacy to the Moment

Immediacy means that you notice a relationship between what the leader talks about "out there" and what actually happens in the moment between the two of you. When you notice this parallel occurrence, you can report your experience *of* her directly *to* her in the here and now. Rather than see yourself as outside of what the leader describes, you put yourself radically within it. This helps the client get a clearer picture of what happens with her in her organization. How you interact with the leader and your internal reactions to her can be useful information. She can assess her effectiveness and identify an area for change.

During your coaching conversations with a client, you increase your ability to bring immediacy by doing these activities:

1. **Scan for parallel occurrences** between the leader's actions in her world and what the leader does with you.
2. **Identify your reactions** to the leader's actions.
3. **Speak directly** *to* **the leader about your experience** *of* **her.**
4. **Make the connection** between your experience of the leader in the moment and the ways she may be doing the same thing elsewhere.

It does not take very long to begin to notice **parallel occurrences.** People often act consistently across contexts, including the conversation with you. The key is to hone in on the occurrences that have the most relevance to the issue at hand. It also requires some attentiveness on the part of the coach.

You know that you are not scanning for parallel occurrences when your mind wanders while you listen to a client's story, and you think it is a waste of time. You miss it if you are thinking, "Okay, so what has this story got to do with anything? She's mentioning her victories again." You *do* start to scan and hone in on parallel occurrences when you think, "Am I the only one whose mind wanders off when she talks? How often does she list off victories with her team, and how is this related to her effect on them?"

Identifying your personal reactions is crucial for immediacy, which is a "here and now" conversation. Your reactions become useful information. That means you focus on what is going on *here*—between you and the other person, not you and someone else, and *now*—at this very moment, not in the past or the future. Here and now conversations often get lost in the organizational world because we focus so often on *there*—everyone and everything else—and *then*—any moment besides now, either the past or the future. Here and now conversations have a lot of power because people do not usually get such direct feedback.

Identifying to yourself the here and now reactions in the scenario mentioned earlier might happen something like this: "So how am I reacting to these stories? I'm not seeing the connection to the topic we are discussing. At first, I resist them and wander off mentally. And now I wonder, why does she do it?"

Once you have identified your reactions, you can do the last two steps. **Tell the leader your direct experience** and **link it to her work world.** You might say, for example, "I hear you talk about your successes, but I'm not seeing the connection to the topic we're discussing. Frankly, I'm starting to wander off. Then I start guessing why you're doing it. Maybe your team tries to second guess you sometimes too."

Of course, you always take a chance when you use immediacy. You could be way off, or too directly on target. You could offend your client. You could scare her off by getting too intense too soon. In the best case, you could catch your client's attention in a new way and engender an invitation from the leader to get more of that kind of feedback from you.

Without using immediacy, it is impossible to get to the heart of some issues. Immediacy helps a client identify her knee-jerk patterns and helps her make new choices. It takes tremendous presence to do this as a coach, using the ability to observe patterns of interaction and reactivity in your client while you are also participating and interacting with her.

When you do have the presence to stop the action of your conversation to report your observations and reactions, you evoke more presence from your client. The trance of her reactivity may break long enough for her to see herself in a new way. This can be a tremendous gift to your client. It requires courage to speak on the part of the coach and courage to listen on the part of the client.

Recently, I experienced the power of using immediacy with a prospective client.

. . . .

Matt

Matt and I were talking about the successes and challenges he felt as a leader of his department in a large national corporation. I admired his strategic thinking. He brought it to every example he gave. I also saw that he seemed relatively satisfied with his efforts in his department, but he sought some indefinable enhancement among the people who worked for him.

After probing in several different ways about the changes and possible outcomes that he wanted, I fell into my own pit. It seemed I had nothing to offer this man, not even a decent diagnosis, because I could not get a handle on what it was that he wanted to be different. There was a ten minute stretch when it may have looked as though I was listening to what he was saying, but I was actually berating myself thinking, "You call yourself a consultant? What business do I have taking up this man's time? How can I gracefully end this appointment?" In other words, I had reached my tolerance level in my discomfort with his vagueness.

Then I paused to regain my bearings. I began to realize that I already was having a significant experience of this leader and I could give him feedback about a pattern I was noticing. It might hint at where he wants to go next. The feedback would be somewhat risky because I did not know him well. It could either end any chance of working with him, or catapult us to a higher degree of interaction and productivity in our prospective working relationship. Well, I was not currently getting anywhere, so I took the risk. I brought my presence forward to the next moment with him.

I said, "Matt, I find your strategic thinking quite valuable. It matches much of my own experience, and therefore I trust your instincts about your company and your department. If I were a direct report of yours, I would like your thinking and be ready to follow it. But I also find that throughout the conversation, I am repeatedly having a second reaction to your strategic thinking. You give no goal, or direction, or action to take after your opinions. So I find myself ready to follow but don't know where to go."

This was the moment of truth. I didn't know whether Matt would bring his own presence to the moment or defend himself against it. In this instance, I was fortunate enough to be with a leader who responded to the invitation to engage on a deeper level.

At first he hesitated and had a puzzled look on his face. Then he said, "Actually, I probably don't take that next step. It's a bit of a risk, and I don't get around to it with either my boss or my staff." In the rest of the conversation, he was able to engage more specifically about this challenge, not only with his department but also with his boss. This allowed us to forge a potential area of coaching work with him to leverage both himself and his department to greater results.

• • • • • • •

This kind of immediate speaking and listening can produce both a frightening and exhilarating moment. When you do the hard work of bringing your presence to a conversation, you break the ground for other tasks. When you do not bring your signature self to these moments, you have the back-breaking job of trying to leverage change in either stubbornly resistant or overly compliant clients.

Parallel Journeys of Executive and Coach

Besides working on bringing your presence and these four approaches to your coaching, one of the greatest contributions you can make is helping the leader find more of her own signature presence. It is the most powerful tool that she brings to her leading.

Leaders are not immune to losing their own resourcefulness. When they become reactive in a situation, it can take on a variety of forms:

- Becoming impatient and demanding when people are resistant to dramatic change

- Giving up their agenda whenever a particular staff member challenges their position

- Seeking endlessly for more information when facing competing factions

- Vacillating between being a rigid dictator and a relaxed teacher

When a leader exhibits any of this kind of reactivity, she has lost the balance between being clear about where she stands and staying connected to those who work with her. When she remains unconscious of this reactivity, she does not seek help but tries the same thing over again. If she becomes aware of the futility of her efforts, she can bring in a coach.

Your job as coach is to **be a resource to help strengthen the leader's presence.** To the extent that you struggle to manage your reactivity and have achieved a greater presence, you have an understanding of what the leader faces in bringing forth her signature presence. You know what some of the journey looks like, both the roadblocks and the opportunities. The leader increases her presence by focusing on the same four approaches to presence that a coach uses. Your agenda with your clients can be **to help them assess their strengths and weaknesses in these four approaches** and assist them in moving toward them: (1) identifying and sustaining a goal, (2) managing themselves in ambiguity, (3) increasing their tolerance for anxiety and reactivity, and (4) using immediacy. The next chapter explores more about the leaders' reactions to stress and how to help them regain their resourcefulness.

. . . .

CHAPTER TWO HIGHLIGHTS

Signs of Signature Presence

1. Bring yourself to the moment with your client.

2. Increase your tolerance for uncomfortable situations.

Self-Differentiation

1. Work to maintain a balance of backbone and heart in your work.

2. Develop quick recovery from reactivity.

Strenghten Your Presence

1. Identify and sustain a goal for yourself in each coaching session.
   - Choose a content and/or process goal.
   - Know your vulnerability in a reactive system.
   - Remember your goal.
   - Be more committed to your goal than easing your discomfort in the moment.

2. Manage yourself in the midst of ambiguity.
   - Acknowledge the ambiguity.
   - Distinguish for yourself when you are clear or unclear about the situation.
   - Articulate to others the boundary of your clarity and lack of clarity.
   - Say what it is you want to do, given the situation.
   - Tell others what you need from them.

3. Increase your tolerance for reactivity within you and around you.
   - Identify the trigger to your reactivity.
   - Learn your typical reaction to that trigger.
   - Choose an alternative response to get you started down a different path.
   - Stay on track with your goal in the session.

4. Bring immediacy to the moment.
   - Scan for parallel occurrences between the leader's actions in her world and what the leader is doing with you.
   - Identify your reaction to the leader's action.
   - Speak directly *to* the leader about your experience *of* her.
   - Make the connection between your experience of the leader and how she may be doing the same thing elsewhere.

Parallel Journeys of Executive and Coach

1. Be a resource for the strengthening of the leader's presence.
2. Help the executive assess her strengths and weaknesses in the four approaches to presence.

• • • • • •

3

• •

Systems Thinking

Understanding Challenges of
the Executive and Coach

This chapter further explores the effects on leaders of dealing with stressful situations and the ways they elicit reactive responses. The chapter emphasizes learning to see those effects and understanding the magnitude of the forces operating in the leader's system. As you read I invite you to see whether you can detect the systems patterns that work on and through your clients. And see whether you can identify what effects these leaders have on you, what ways they alter how you work with your clients. Attending closely to the ideas presented here—key systems concepts—will give you a new way to see the forces that create an impact on and through you, your clients, and their organizations. Seeing with new eyes gives you greater choices when you face the challenges brought to you by your clients.[1]

• • • • • • •

A Typical Story
Tom and Ben, Executive and Coach

Tom is a senior vice president of finance in a company where he has worked for fifteen years. The company, part of an industry that has been pretty staid over the last forty years, has made money without a lot of effort. Now the industry is rapidly changing and requires aggressive entrepreneurship on the part of the company, which is unprepared for this adjustment. A new chief executive officer, Susan, has been hired from the outside and has the move-forward vision and energy that the board knows it needs. Susan tells Tom that the sleepy way he has run finance is no longer acceptable. The monthly accounting report dates have to be moved up by a week, the department has to show a 30 percent reduction in operating costs, and she expects Tom to come up with the plan to get there.

Tom is anxious about the demands in these mandates. He has never pushed his people before. He avoids conflict at all costs. Tom turns to Ben for help. Ben is the internal organization development specialist for the company.

· · · · · · ·

Tom, rather unexpectedly, has found himself in hot water and off balance. Everything is changing around him: the business environment, his new boss, different expectations.

How can Ben coach Tom effectively? If you were Ben, what would you do? How does Ben approach such an anxious executive, one who experiences himself as being under siege? What framework can Ben bring to this coaching relationship so that he can stay on course himself?

Ben can use a systems perspective. This chapter explores the second principle from Chapter One, the usefulness of a systems framework for executive coaches. Using this perspective keeps coaches focused on the fundamental processes either promoting or impeding their work with leaders.

Specifically, I am using the systems thinking from the family systems field and applying it to organizations. I have found it to be one of the most powerful lenses to use in viewing business issues. Although I neither use the specific techniques of that field nor attempt to make therapeutic interventions, I apply this way of *thinking* to organizations.

A systems perspective resists identifying one element or person in a system as the root cause of a problem. A system can guide the actions of individuals and has greater staying power than the specific personalities of individuals or the mission and goals of the organization. Following are a handful of concepts of the world of systems. (These concepts, and those in Chapter Four, drive the methodology in Chapters Five through Eight.)

The Interactional Force Field

When any two or ten or hundred people interact with one another over time, they create a **social interactional field.**[2] It operates through the relationships of those involved, but it has a character, shape, and set of rules transcending any individual.

A spider web is a good metaphor to describe an interactional force field. When anything comes into contact with a spider web, anywhere on its surface, the whole web moves. If anything shakes or disrupts the attachment points of the web, the web moves. This resiliency of the web is one of its greatest assets. The ability to be strong yet flexible allows the web to maintain its integrity through many disruptions—wind, rain, or flying insects. Spider webs are often invisible to the observer, yet they go on functioning in their interplay of movement and stability. Webs also have their breaking point. A web can be disturbed or torn to such an extent that it is destroyed, thus losing its integrity, beauty, and identity.

So it is with an interactional field established between two or more people. It has its own anchor points, resiliency, and breaking point. It is most often invisible to the members within it. When anyone within the field moves, all members feel the effect, though differently, based on their positions. Other images of an interactional field are the field of gravity and the magnetic field. We are immersed within their invisible force, yet we feel their influence.

Say a group of three people are in a meeting with their boss. Person A reports on his week's activities. Person B gazes out the window. Person C writes notes in her binder. Person D, the boss, asks questions of Person A.

Before I continue, I invite you to choose one of the people in this scenario whose actions you are most likely to duplicate in a similar circumstance. In the setting of a routine business meeting, do you identify with Person A, B, C, or D? Is this because you are by nature conscientious (A), or bored at meetings (B), able to do multiple tasks (C), or show interest in the topic at hand (D)?

Now, imagine the boss's boss, Person E, walking into the room unannounced. How are the players likely to react? How is your character likely to react? Do they continue doing exactly what they were doing before? Usually, the answer is no. Every person in the room gets organized in a new way because of the introduction of another variable, Person E, the boss's boss. No one stopped the meeting. No one changed the agenda. No one's personality was suddenly altered. Yet all kinds of things have perceptibly shifted.

Let's say that note-taking Person C is a new employee who just started that day. She has never met Person E and does not know he is the boss's boss. She experiences the invisible field by witnessing the change in behavior of the other three people. Like the needle of a compass pointing north, the new employee is starting to shift toward the direction of the others' change in behavior to learn what this magnetic force is all about. The members of the meeting reorganize themselves without explaining any new rules to her or to each other. Yet the effect is immediate and obvious.

Interactional fields take on a life of their own, even as individuals in an organization come and go. I once worked for a restaurant that maintained the same level of service and quality through several years. Though they aspired to be "world class," they were good, but not exceptional. The managers and 70 percent of the staff left and newcomers took their place. The force field remained the same: good but not excellent. There were factors in place affecting the system that were more enduring than the individuals within it.

Seeing the Force Field

How do I learn about the interactional field? How can I begin to see it? You can watch for and notice the different ways that you show up in various groups and the effect that the system has on you. Say, for example, you fly from Chicago to Boston with Cattle Call Airlines. Just flying with CCA sets your teeth on edge because, among other things, the employees do not smile. They just go through the motions, the food service is slow, and they never look you in the eye. You are crabby and tired when you arrive in Boston.

In contrast, the Chicago to Boston flight of Peak Service Airlines is completely different. PSA employees smile, act as though they like their coworkers, and deliver service efficiently, on time, and with welcoming friendliness. You leave the flight calm and contented. Same flight time, same kind of airplane. But the web created by each of these systems calls out different responses in you.

When people talk about the "feel" of the place, they are noticing the web created by the system's field. When you notice that you are having distinctly different feelings and thoughts and motivations just by virtue of being in two different organizations, you are experiencing the interactional field.

Yes, but now you may say, *I can see what you're saying sometimes, especially when I am a customer, but often I have the same experiences no matter where I go! For instance, no matter what organization I work for, I always wind up being the unsung hero who works too hard, saves the day at the last minute, and feels burnt out afterward. My experience is—all work systems are alike!*

In an uncanny way, organizations seek individuals to fulfill the same roles they have always had for certain positions or in particular departments (unsung hero, watchdog, cheerleader, underachiever, and so forth). You may be selected for your ability to be an unsung hero over and over again because the systems employing you know a hero when they see one. Also in an uncanny way, you seek out organizations that welcome you into the hero role.

You probably learned to be an unsung hero from your first organization, your family. Families develop their own interactional fields shaping the experiences of those within them. Consequently, systems interlock with each other. You take the interactional field from your family with you when you step inside your work organization. This can lead to you having the same experiences everywhere you go because the different systems bring forth the same response from you, the one you have been trained to give.

What do these interactional webs have to do with coaching? Practically everything! First, it is critical to **know how organizational systems affect you—the ones you are in and co-create.** Reactivity (see Chapter Two) also shows where you are particularly vulnerable in a system and respond with knee-jerk habits. When you maintain a self-differentiated presence you can feel the effects of a system but avoid reacting automatically. The more you develop the four approaches to presence, the greater is your effectiveness in maintaining your equilibrium in the system's force field.[3]

Second, it is equally important to **attend to the system co-created between you and your client. Within interactional fields, people establish ways of relating that become like choreographed dance patterns over time. These patterns are either useful or counterproductive.** Typical client-coach patterns include a wide variety of behaviors. Here is a sample of them (the first two are useful, the second two less effective):

- Client seeks advice: coach fosters independent thinking.

- Client seeks tough feedback: coach gives it.

- Client vents: coach placates.

- Client is continually late for appointments: coach tolerates it.

Every relationship develops a systems "dance," and the coach-client relationship is no different. It is important to take an inventory and figure out the types of dances you develop with different kinds of clients. Can you name the typical patterns of interrelating that you and your clients develop over time? Are these patterns effective for your clients and your coaching?

Third, it is important to begin to **see the system the leader is in.** Often, the very pattern developing between you and the executive is a living sample of the system your client is in with his own organization. Systems have a way of extending themselves out to their farthest boundaries, pulling anyone who comes close to them into their interactional vortex.

In the following example I discovered my client's system by paying attention to how she interacted with me.

♦ ♦ ♦ ♦ ♦ ♦ ♦

Joanne

Joanne was like two different people. Part of the time she seemed relaxed and unhurried. In fact, she was not focused enough to make any progress. Although she never said it, she seemed to have an attitude of, "Don't worry about it; it'll take care of itself." When we had our sessions, she treated them like friendly chats. In contrast, she would call out of the blue, hurried and intense, needing to see me immediately to settle an emerging situation. She wanted resolution of the issue and she asked (or insisted) I make sessions with her a priority in my work life.

♦ ♦ ♦ ♦ ♦ ♦ ♦

Like Joanne, the organization spasmed from a laid-back atmosphere of high sociability to a five-alarm fire emergency response. My client was one of the high-ranking executives who perpetrated this dichotomy of energy. Even though the project she was addressing with me did not require these two energies, they seeped through anyway. The more you take your working relationship with your client as a learning lab of the system, the more you can help your client see the system's pull on her and her influence on it.

It is not surprising that you, as a coach, get pulled into the system's self-perpetuating patterns. This is both a blessing and a curse. The benefit is that you get a first-hand knowledge of what it is like for your client to live in that system. You start experiencing the same gut reactions of people in the system. The problem is, well, that you have the same gut reactions of people in the system. The larger perspective you bring to your client can begin to diminish. This is why understanding how systems work, identifying their fields, and breaking out of unproductive patterns is so essential to coaches.

In summary, you can learn to see the interactional field's effect on your coaching by

- Getting to know your vulnerability points in a system, where and when you get reactive.

- Identifying the client-coach dances you co-create.

- Uncovering the system's pull on the leader by observing how she is reacting to you.

The Effect of Anxiety in the Workplace

When a stable interactional force field (whether it is a work team, a family, or an entire organization) encounters a challenge or disruption too large for its own resiliency, the people within it experience heightened anxiety. Some examples of large disruptions include

- The company being sold to another company

- A boss leaving and one replacing him

- Market forces signaling a shift

Anxiety jams the normal, comfortable way of acting in a system and causes a variety of reactions:

- Resistance

- Blaming

- Reorganization

- Self-protection

- Loss of creativity

- Heroic efforts

Moments of anxiety seriously challenge the leader's ability to bring his presence to a business situation.

The use of the term *anxiety* does not refer to its everyday use, the kind of natural anxiety people get when they are trying out a new skill or the nervousness that comes with giving a presentation. In fact, some degree of anxiety is productive for learning, indicating we are on the edge of our known skills and are about to launch into new territory.

I am using *anxiety* more technically as referring to a response a person and/or a system has to forces that stretch them toward a potential breaking point or a *perceived* breaking point. Anxiety is the early-warning device to alert the system to counter with a system-preserving reaction, usually fight or flight.

When anxiety throws people off balance they become reactive, an unproductive automatic response to forces around them. They lose their creative response to a situation. It is the difference between overturning a boat while white water rafting or successfully navigating through the rapids.

Other major factors besides anxiety affect leaders and systems: the skills of people in the organization, their capabilities, motivations, and contributions. These factors must be assessed when evaluating an organization or a leader's ability to achieve business goals.

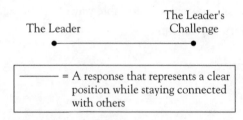

Figure 3.1. The Leader's Response in Low-Stress Situations.

However, even the most skilled, capable, motivated, and insightful people muffle their effectiveness if they do not address the power of the system and their unique vulnerability to its pull on them.

Therefore, in low-stress situations where a talented leader's anxiety is also low, she meets challenges well. She can accomplish the two critical tasks of leadership: (1) leading with backbone (taking clear positions on issues) *while at the same time* (2) leading with heart (staying connected to the people who work with her) (see Figure 3.1).

The Leader's Challenge

When the external challenge escalates and, what is more important, when the leader's reactivity to the situation increases, it creates an internal tension. Her anxiety reaches a level that floods her normal responses. This puts a breaker either on her ability to take clear positions, or to stay connected to her staff, or both (Figure 3.2).

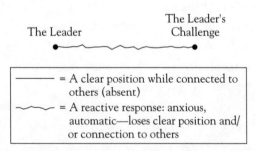

Figure 3.2. The Leader's Anxiety While Under Increased Stress.

How can you tell whether the executive you are working with is falling into her knee-jerk reaction? The symptoms can widely vary. Essentially, you can tell it has happened when she has lost the ability either to be clear and/or to be connected to others. Many possible thoughts, feelings, and desires can operate when someone experiences reactive anxiety. Here are a few possibilities, some of which you may have heard from your clients:

The Executive's Internal Voices While Anxious

- I don't have a clue what to do now.

- Why don't they just do what I want them to do?

- I have lost track of how to prioritize all the variables.

- I'll do the first thing that comes to mind.

- If they understood how complex this is, they'd stop whining about it.

- Maybe someone else will know what to do.

- I'll look for a magic bullet.

- I'm so mad I just want to lash out.

- How did I get into this mess in the first place?

- They let me down again—I can never depend on them.

- I'll probably lose my job over this.

- I always have to go it alone.

Catastrophic, "either/or" thinking, with "always" and "never" thrown in, is a sure sign that the leader is in the throes of her reactive thinking-action patterns. Essentially, she has lost access to her internal resources and resilience. She has unknowingly disengaged from herself. This is a sign of the depth of the problem and also a key to its resolution. She can regain her presence by balancing backbone and heart (the key), but she has difficulty locating the key because it is buried under all her reactivity.

Triangles—Whose Stress Is This, Anyway?

One response to anxiety is involving a third person to relieve some of the pressure the individual experiences between himself and the challenge he feels (the challenge could be a person, an issue, or a group of people). This creates a triangle of involvement between the initial person, his challenge, and the third person. Triangles are often created unconsciously to lower stress. Sometimes turning to a third person is a good tactic. It helps the anxious person collect his thinking and reapproach the challenge with renewed energy. Often, however, the move to the third person prolongs the unresolved situation.

There are many triangles in life. Some of the most frequently occurring ones are

Anxious Person	Is Challenged By	And Turns To
wife	husband	child
parent	child	teacher
husband	wife	in-laws
manager	employee	HR department
customer service rep.	customer	vendor
salesperson	inventory manager	production supervisor

Leaders also use triangles when under stress. An example of triangulation occurs in the story at the beginning of this chapter. Tom, the senior vice president of finance, is the anxious one, and Susan is his challenge. Tom becomes disturbed about the relationship he has with Susan and the demands she places on him.

To relieve his anxiety, Tom turns to Ben, the internal organizational specialist, and involves him in the Tom-Susan work relationship (Figure 3.3).

You have probably witnessed leaders doing this in work relationships. There are many ways that Tom could triangle someone else into his relationship with Susan. Some of the possibilities are the following (the first two feed anxiety; the third one addresses it productively):

- Tom could use one of his staff members as a confidante to complain about Susan. (*Tom says to staff person:* "*Can you believe what Susan did in the meeting this morning? It just shows you how out of it she is about our situation.*")

- Tom could create an alliance with Susan by turning another senior VP into a common adversary. (*Tom says to Susan:* "*Last Spring Jack said my department was running at peak efficiency. If I had known how far off he was,*

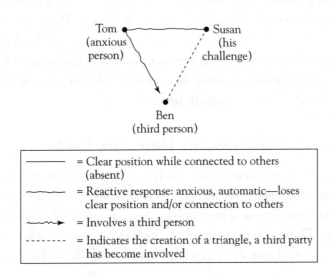

Figure 3.3. Triangulation.

> *I would have come to you as soon as you took the job to see how we could solve the problem.")*

- Tom could go to human resources (HR) to help him work through how to approach Susan. *(Tom says to HR director: "Susan and I don't see eye to eye at all on this one. Can you help me figure out what we're really disagreeing about? I've been over and over it with her, and we keep covering the same ground. I need a fresh perspective.")*

The possibilities are endless. Do these reactions sound familiar? The first two examples show how we try everything we can to throw off our anxiety, to get rid of it, build walls around it, pass it on to someone else, or hide from it. It is as though we are allergic to our own anxiety. When in the hot seat of stress, we will go to great lengths to distract ourselves away from the anxiety that is fueling our distress.

Even Tom's own internal voices—his anger, worries, fears, and disappointments—are distractions that keep him from focusing on the monumental task of the external challenge. These voices are like internal triangles, ways to lock up or siphon off the leader's energy rather than allowing him to focus on the challenge at hand. The *real* challenge is having the courage to stay focused on the situation and what it requires in terms of a response.

Signs That Triangles Are Distracting Leaders

The leader's reactivity often involves multiple parties and creates multiple triangles in an attempt to resolve anxiety. Reactivity can cascade throughout a system—by requests, new rules, demands, gossip. These reactions drain the system of creative resources to solve the problem. Here is what happens with Tom (Figure 3.4).

• • • • • • •

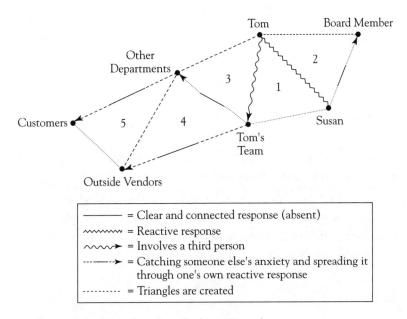

Figure 3.4. Cascading, Interlocking Triangles.

Tom and Ben, continued

Before talking with Ben, Tom tells his team what Susan has said. He paints the picture in such a way that an image of Susan develops as the evil disruptive force from outside (triangle 1). Members of the department become very upset and talk about the company letting them down. They rally to Tom's side, sympathizing about the terrible pressure he must be under. After the meeting, the department's gossip grapevine feeds the team's anxiety about their job security, fuels resentment about having to change procedures, and speculates that Tom probably is not standing up for their interests with Susan (triangles are multiplying).

In senior VP team meetings with Susan, Tom is silent during the brainstorming discussions on models for restructuring. Susan becomes irritated with Tom's lack of action and starts wondering and talking with a board member, wondering about replacing him (triangle 2). Tom's team, in their distraction with the turmoil in their department, starts missing deadlines with other departments (triangle 3) and outside vendors (triangle 4), thus affecting the service the company's customers are receiving in delivery of goods and timeliness of invoices (triangle 5).

• • • • • • •

When other people become reactive to the situation, the leader, or each other, the system loses its flexibility to deal with the challenging situation. It freezes and locks. In this case, the executive's reactivity can become the organizing center of all the triangles, creating an anxiety vortex. <u>Anxiety becomes the distraction rather than the motivator to go to the creative source, the leader's own resilience. The number one priority, and a goal of your coaching, is to help the executive get back to that creative center.</u>

Enter the Coach

When leaders become reactive to their own challenges, they may turn to a coach to help them out of their quagmire. This relationship can create a healthy triangle between the leader and his dilemma. It helps the leader to work toward regaining his balance and returning to more constructive work relationships (Figure 3.5).

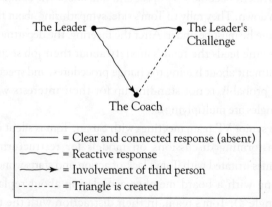

Figure 3.5. The Triangled Coach.

This is exactly what Tom does. He finds the situation so anxiety producing that he approaches Ben for help. Triangles can have either a stabilizing effect on a system or a debilitating one. As a stabilizer, a triangle gives anxiety a temporary place to reside while the leader chooses a thoughtful next step. If Tom does this as a way to clear his own thinking so he can choose a course of action, turning to Ben is a healthy use of a triangle.

If Tom goes to Ben in an attempt to avoid his situation, he will remain reactive and get less out of his sessions with Ben. Who has not first tried to get out of a tough situation before truly dealing with it? A coach's beginning relationship with clients often involves the client wanting to download the problem rather than to face it, and coaches need to watch for this propensity when entering the coaching triangle.

Your position as coach within the multiple triangles is a powerful one, and you can use it to help break the frozen state of the system. **Your job is to assist the executive in recovering his resilience and resources.** Paradoxically, you need to enter the triangle in such a way that you *stay out of the way*. You do not want the executive to continue siphoning off his energy to you, but to turn back to his own temporarily suppressed resilience.

• • • • • • •

Tom and Ben, continued

Ben is thinking, "Tom is spawning triangles throughout his entire system. They're just digging him further into his hole. And he's got his eye out for Susan like a rabbit has its eye out for roving dogs. What he needs is to become more of the master of his destiny rather than a victim of it." Ben believes that what may be most useful to Tom is refocusing him on his goals and how Susan's mandates fit into those goals. That would be the place to start, with a close second being increasing Tom's ability to manage himself in the midst of all this ambiguity.

• • • • • • •

This is easier said than done. When an executive under stress turns to a coach for help, one of several **central patterns** occurs between client and coach:

1. The executive retains ownership of his challenge and uses the coach as a sounding board to clear his thinking and set some goals.

2. The executive attempts to off-load his anxiety onto the coach, but the coach refuses to take responsibility for the problem.

3. The executive off-loads his anxiety onto the coach, who works harder than the client to relieve the client of stress.

The first option is a great experience with a mature client. The second is effective when the coach can stay firm and compassionate with the leader. As for the third, interactions between an executive and a coach can be off and running and well down the road before either realizes they have been operating in the third mode. This pattern temporarily relieves the leader of stress but gives him no more ability to solve his own challenges.

The third path happens more times than coaches—myself included—would like to admit. Therefore, the task at hand is learning the patterns you play out when you get stressed by anxious clients. It is good to ask yourself, *How does this dance get started? Why didn't I see it coming in the first place?* Though you may want to know what to *do* in these situations, you cannot take effective action until you learn your side of the pattern.

Patterns—Shall We Dance?

Patterns are either useful or counterproductive depending on whether they contribute to people achieving their goals.[4] These patterns are suprarational, meaning they exist beyond a logical process of how people plan or intend to relate. An unconscious system reinforces itself and calls on both parties to adapt to it and perpetuate it.

It is difficult not to attribute these patterns to the intrapsychic process of one individual. Actually, they are snapshots of the system as a whole. It is truly a dance—the constant moving and adapting together that makes or breaks graceful movement. There are endless variations of two-person patterns. The following provide a representative sample:

- One pursues and the other distances.

- One attacks and the other defends.

- One underachieves and the other overachieves.

- One initiates and the other follows.

Both partners contribute equally to creating the seamless (though sometimes stormy) flow of their relating.

Key questions can help you discover patterns you have with your clients.

- What dances do you develop with which kinds of clients?

- Can you name them?

- Do they largely fall into dance 1, 2, or 3 of the basic options?

- Are these patterns effective for you and your clients?

Say you find yourself recognizing the third option—taking on the executive's burden (overachieving while she underachieves)—with some of your coaching clients. It takes courage to admit to being a co-creator of this pattern. It can happen so subtly. One way of testing for it is to ask the following:

- Who is working harder to figure out and solve the problem, you or the leader?

- Who's sleeping better at night? (You're in trouble if it's not you.)

- Which calls from clients do you dread?

- Who requires a higher energy level because being with them takes a lot out of you?

When you answer these questions, you may realize that you are taking more ownership of your client's stress than is useful for either of you.

What forces create this pattern between the leader and coach? Why does it seem so hard to get out of it with some clients? Let's take a closer look at the system created between an executive and a coach.

The Coach's Challenge

Remember the strength of an interactional field: systems extend themselves out to their edges, pulling you into their vortex. As I mentioned before, coaches can catch the system's anxiety. As a coach, you can lose access to your own strengths and resources, just as the leader has lost his.

Coaches are not immune to anxious moments, especially while facing the anxiety and reactivity of their clients. This is why it takes fortitude to withstand being with an anxious leader. If anyone sits long enough with someone who is anxious, it will eventually get on their nerves (after, say, twenty minutes or, . . . what is your limit?). Anxiety, left to its own devices, spreads and multiplies quickly through a system. Leaders do not need coaches to be anxiety "step-up transformers" for them. They are surrounded by enough people who do that already.

A cluster of anxiety-producing circumstances can cause coaches to become reactive and lose their bearings. To which of these circumstances are you susceptible?

1. You enter the interactional field of the executive, which is characterized by high anxiety and reactivity.
2. The executive has lost a sense of his resources, has become rudderless.
3. He is looking to you to save him and believes that you have the resources he wishes he had.
4. You have bought into the anxious belief that it is your responsibility to rescue him.

The last one is the clincher. When these circumstances are combined, I get temporary amnesia about my own resources and competence. I get caught in the interactional field of the leader's anxiety, which steps up my reactivity to his anxiety.

Sometimes the messages I give myself are tip-offs to this anxious state. Here are a few of my personal favorites. You may have some of your own.

The Coach's Internal Voices While Anxious

- The leader looks to me for help, and I haven't a clue what to offer.

- Advice comes out of my mouth, and even I don't buy it.

- He just doesn't get it.

- He isn't taking my advice.

- I'll do the first thing that comes to mind.

- I'll just prioritize these items for him.

- I'm intimidated by the leader.

- I'm not giving him his money's worth.

- I'm working with a leader who doesn't have what it takes.

- How did I get into this situation in the first place?

- I'm taking sides between the leader and his team.

- I can't stand the discomfort he is in—maybe Herculean efforts on my part will save him from his dilemma.

Sometimes when I coach, I am so focused on the leader's anxiety and my reactivity to his anxiety, I pay no attention to my own resilience and creativity. When anxious, coaches become less available to themselves and therefore lose their creative thinking with the leader.

Have you ever had those days when a client pours out his troubles to you and they are *huge?* They are real problems, a challenge for the wisdom of King Solomon himself. Then, with his desperate eyes staring at you, he falls silent, waiting for a response. Sometimes clients' hand-wringing over their dilemmas can be contagious. I feel on the spot to come up with *the answer*. I grasp at giving advice, using techniques, or cheerleading. Though I do not admit it, I do this to lower my own anxiety, or at least to distract myself from my discomfort. Worse still, I rationalize to myself that I am being useful to my client.

Your internal voices can distract you from your central task—being in relationship to an anxious leader who has lost *his* resources. If you are not careful, you can become a substitute player for the leader in his organization, where suddenly you as the coach are the organizing principle in the system. That is what happens with Ben as he works with Tom.

• • • • • • •

Tom and Ben, continued

Ben is taken aback when Tom, in their next session, tells him not to tell anyone that he (Ben) is coaching him on this problem (secrets are another form of triangulating). Tom is embarrassed about needing help and doesn't want to appear weak in front of the other senior VPs and especially Susan. His job may be on the line if he doesn't pull this off well and soon.

Tom's request for secrecy increases Ben's anxiety. He has his own stake in this. He wants Susan to respect him for the help he can give her and others in resolving business challenges. She doesn't have a lot of patience for team processes that go on and on with few results. Since Susan is new, she has yet to see what value Ben brings to organizational issues.

Ben feels as pressured as Tom to produce results. He's torn and finds it difficult to identify his first priority and his primary client. He figures he can either coach Tom in his development, or get on Susan's reorganization train (his growing reactivity presents these two options as polarized). His response to Tom is, "Hey, don't worry about it. Let's get right down to business and figure out a reorganization plan for your department."

Ben alleviates some of Tom's anxiety by managing the reorganization strategy, not that he officially has this designation. Tom is the up-front lead of course, but Ben is in essence supervising Tom's efforts. Ben tells Tom to schedule team meetings. Ben facilitates getting the team's ideas at these meetings and collates the information for Tom.

Tom shows Ben a memo from Susan, requesting a revised organization chart in two weeks. Ben sets up a timeline of activities for Tom to follow so he will meet the two-week deadline. Team members individually approach Ben (more triangles) with their concerns about the new structure, as well as concerns about Tom's ability to manage the new structure. Ben works harder to find a structure that would suit Tom's abilities and the interests of the team, as well as satisfying Susan's parameters.

· · · · · · ·

As you can see by this story, something insidious happens when the coach takes on the executive's burden. He stops believing the leader is capable. One of the core tenets of coaching is the belief that a leader has his own resourcefulness to face his dilemmas. That resourcefulness could mean seeking assistance from a coach. The help, however, supports the executive in facing the issue and seeing it through.

When you lose faith in the executive's ability to lead, you have also actually lost faith in your ability to coach an anxious leader. True coaching requires standing in the uncomfortable crucible of the leader's anxiety without stepping in and doing his job for him. The vacuum you create by a loss of faith in yourself and the leader pulls a kind of pseudo-help out of you. It may have short-term benefits but does not make a more resilient executive in the long run.

Once you identify your own reactive dance, the next step is to have a way of thinking through your role in the triangle. Once you see how you can act powerfully within it, you will unlock your own ability and creativity to generate effective interventions. Chapter Four offers just such a model.

• • • • • • •

CHAPTER THREE HIGHLIGHTS

Systems Perspective Useful to Coaches

1. Learn to see the interactional fields and your vulnerability within them.

2. Identify the coach-client dances you co-create.

3. See the system that surrounds and is co-created by the leader.

The Effect of Anxiety in the Workplace

1. Learn to distinguish productive anxiety from a reactive response to system challenges.

2. Look for triangles the leader creates.

3. Learn to identify the cascading effects of triangles throughout a system.

4. Anticipate being triangled by the leader into his dilemma.

The Coach's Challenge

1. Help the executive recover his resilience.

2. Work to keep from taking on the client's burden.

• • • • • • •

. . . .

The Triangled Coach

Being Effective in the Middle

If you have ever had the experience of working harder than your client on his problem, you know viscerally when you have veered off track. Putting out more effort than the leader, as Ben is doing with Tom, does little to build the leader's ability to face challenges. Executive coaches need a way of working in the *leader–leader's challenge–coach* triangle that keeps the coach in the coach role and the leader in the leader role.

The following, contrasting models outline critically different paths coaches take while functioning within this triangle. I invite you to avoid the Rescue Model and use the Client Responsibility Model. The latter provides a guiding theme to keep you on track while the leader's anxiety buffets you. When you start questioning your actions, this model can help you return to home base, where you can make clearer choices.

Note: The juxtaposition and contrast of models for coaching in the business environment (named here the Rescue Model and the Client Responsibility Model) are the invention of Rob Schachter, senior consultant at LIOS Consulting Corporation. Schachter bases his approach on the seminal theory of Murray Bowen and the expansion of Bowen's work by Edwin Friedman.

The Rescue Model and the Client Responsibility Model of Coaching

The less effective approach is appropriately named the **Rescue Model** because the coach takes on the leader's burden. In the Rescue Model the coach enters as the "pseudo" leader of the situation. This can temporarily ease the anxiety of the executive. As a Rescue Model coach you develop relationships with the leader and even the leader's team, issue, or boss that foster dependency on you for the solution. You can become so central that the leader's own relationship to the issue is weakened and takes a back seat (Figure 4.1). When you take ownership of the issue and lead the process to solution, including facilitating, training, setting guidelines, advising, and making decisions *(for example, Ben's "supervising" of Tom)*, you develop strong relationships with the leader and with the team (if you are also working with them). The leader and his team stop developing a relationship with each other.

In contrast, as a **Client Responsibility** coach, you use your position in the triangle to surface information about the system. Then the leader and the rest of the system can regain use of their own resources and continue to relate to each other. You take a back seat

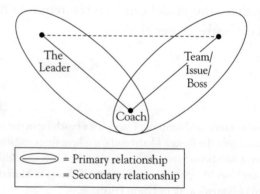

Figure 4.1. Rescue Model of Coaching.

and do not come between the leader and his team, issue, or boss. Your actions ensure that the integrity of those relationships remains intact (Figure 4.2).

As a coach you may still include activities of facilitating, training, and advising, but the *leader* owns the process, the solution, and the decisions. The Client Responsibility Model respects the fact that the coach is secondary to the situation and not a primary player. You work alongside and in partnership with your client.

In the Rescue Model, the problems resurface when you leave. In the Client Responsibility Model, the leader and the team have strengthened their competency to move through their work issues without your presence. It may seem obvious the Client Responsibility Model is more effective for the client. However, we consultants and coaches fall into the Rescue Model often when succumbing to our own anxiety in the face of the leader's distress.

How do I know I am in one mode as opposed to the other? Two areas to watch for are your attitude and your actions. Note in Table 4.1 the contrast in attitudes and behaviors between the two models.

The Client Responsibility Model can help you work within the triangle effectively. The goal is to use your signature presence to keep the leader focused.

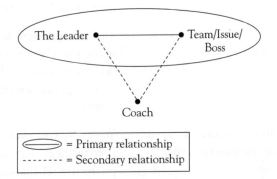

Figure 4.2. Client Responsibility Model of Coaching.

Table 4.1. Contrasts Between Coaching Models.

	Rescue Model	Client Responsibility Mode
Attitudes	You think the leader cannot do it without you.	You believe that the leader has to come up with approaches she is comfortable with rather than adopting yours.
	You find yourself looking over your client's shoulder because you are worried she will blow it.	You know that you are a "short-timer" here, and the leader is the one who has to live with her results.
	You know you would do a better job than the leader.	You accept that a "good enough" action by a highly committed and motivated leader is ten times better than an outstanding action on your part that creates passivity in your client.
	You focus on the executive's weaknesses.	You focus on the executive's strengths.
Behaviors	You give more answers than ask clarifying questions.	You stimulate your client's thinking so that she knows more about her own position.
	You make decisions for the leader.	You seek opportunities to invite your client to be decisive and to articulate clearly her decisions to others.
	You consistently take up more air time than your client.	You invite your client to keep tuned in and stay in a productive relationship with her team.

Let's check back with Ben and backtrack to the moment before he lost his balance and fell into the Rescue Model of coaching. Tom asked him to keep a secret, which triggered Ben's reactivity. If, instead, Ben maintained access to his resilience, he could help Tom get back to *his* resources. Ben's use of the Client Responsibility Model with Tom could look something like this:

. . . .

Tom and Ben, continued

Ben says to Tom, "Tom, you *are* in trouble. But spending your time and my time hiding from this fact isn't going to do you any good. What I *could* do is help you think through a number of serious questions you need to answer for yourself. Have you decided to stay and meet this challenge, or leave? Are you up for this big of a change in how you do things? If you decide to stay, how does this challenge fit into the goals you have for yourself? What does successfully fulfilling those goals look like?"

. . . .

If Tom welcomes the stimulation and challenge from these questions, he has a chance to choose his response, becoming less automatic in his situation. He is also less likely to depend on Ben for answers. Given more coaching sessions, here are other questions Ben can ask Tom:

- How can you find a way to talk to your team so they understand that you stand behind this challenge?

- What parameters can you give your team for a new organization? What information do you know now that you can share with them?

- What information do you require from them?

- What other resources do you need from Susan, from your peers, and from me to get the results you want?

- What challenges in how you manage do you need to address?

- What strengths in your management style and in your team do you want to preserve?

These are the beginning conversations that would help Tom become self-directed in the driver's seat. When you as coach remain in the Client Responsibility Model, you strengthen the leader's ability in the four approaches to presence—staying focused on a goal, managing ambiguity, dealing with reactivity, and becoming more immediate with the staff.

The occupational hazard of coaching from the middle is to get into the kind of difficulty that Ben did with his Rescue Model coaching—stepping in and "supervising" the leader. I have been in Ben's shoes more times than I even know. I continue to work on the goal of being present with my clients so I can withstand their anxiety—not catch it from them, not abandon them in their anxiety, and not be thrown off course when my approach may not look like help to them in the moment. This kind of calm presence in the middle can be enormously useful to leaders seeking answers to their organizational dilemmas.

However, sometimes moving too fast into the Client Responsibility Model can be jarring for a highly anxious leader. This happened with one of my clients.

• • • • • • •

Jill

Jill, a director of human resources, came into our meeting quite harried about an emerging situation with Alan, the purchaser for the production plant, and his boss, Bob, the accounting director. Bob had set some strong guidelines for Alan that he did not like. Alan went to Bob's boss, Carl, the plant manager, and complained bitterly about Bob. Carl had his own doubts about Bob's ability to manage his people. Then Carl came to Jill, hoping she could be a mediator between Alan and his boss, Bob. Jill breathlessly came to me to ask whether I would be willing to mediate a conversation between the two (see Figure 4.3).

. . . .

Here is another excellent example of cascading, interlocking triangles that multiply because of people's anxiety about their own relationships to each other. Alan is upset with his working relationship with his boss, Bob. Alan brings Bob's boss, Carl, into his relationship with Bob. Carl has his own issues with Bob, which he has not satisfactorily addressed. Carl pulls Jill into his relationship to Bob and Bob's relationship with Alan. Jill is nervous about the way Carl uses her in these situations, and so she pulls me into her relationship to Carl, which could ricochet me into the middle of the originating triangle among Alan, Bob, and Carl. Being in the middle is a minefield!

The spreading triangles throw a smoke screen over issues of accountability and authority. Carl needs to deal with Bob directly

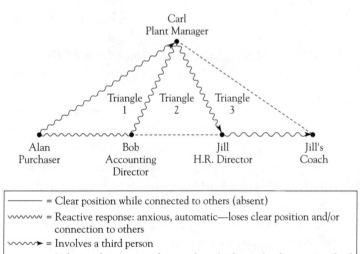

Figure 4.3. The "Hot" Triangles Entangling Jill.

about Carl's issues with Bob's leadership. Bob has to act on the legitimate expectations he has of Alan. Instinctively I knew that the last thing this system needed was for me to join the long chain of triangles.

· · · · · · ·

Jill, continued

With the best of intentions but too quickly I said (matching Jill's breathlessness), "Getting someone from the outside doesn't make any sense. Let's look at how you could be a resource." It sounds logical and helpful and comes out of the Client Responsibility Model of coaching. However, my own anxiety about getting caught in the middle fueled my response.

Jill must have smelled my skittishness. She said that she was irritated with me and rightly so. It seemed as though I was dropping her like a hot potato. My own anxiety was rebuffing her anxious request too quickly. If she were in touch with her own resourcefulness at the time, she would not have turned to me in the first place. Actually, this would have been the perfect time to take the bull by the horns (decisively give her what she wants) and then hand it back again (her own leadership). It might have looked something like this:

"Jill, I would be happy to be a mediator if that is what you most need. Let's take a look at the whole picture and talk through the best course of action."

Jill was able to tell me that she was not feeling confident or resourceful. We slowed down and took a look at the situation more neutrally, talking through the triangles (see Figure 4.4). As her coach, I was able to direct her focus to how she could first work on her approach to Carl (#1) to help realign his relationship with Bob (#2), which had implications for how Carl would more immediately respond to Alan (#3). By the end of the session, Jill did not feel a need for an outside mediator.

· · · · · · ·

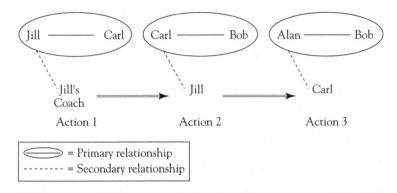

Figure 4.4. Client Responsibility Approach: Actions to Take in Sequence.

Jill calmed down enough in our conversation to regain her own creativity. Her clarity of thinking about the situation returned. She felt much more grounded, found her backbone, and saw what her position should be with Carl (that a mediator was not necessary for Alan and Bob if Carl communicated his expectations to Bob about Bob's leadership, and Carl communicated to Alan that he needed to go back to Bob and work out their conflict). This result—helping the client calm down and get clear about her position and action plan—is one indicator that you are acting from the Client Responsibility position.

In summary, here are the actions you can take as a coach to remain most effective with your clients when you are brought into the middle of the triangle of their relationship to their challenge:

- **Identify and avoid Rescue Model attitudes and behaviors.**

- **Use the attitudes and behaviors of the Client Responsibility Model—sustain a belief in your client's resourcefulness.**

- Support the primary relationship between the
  executive and her challenge, whatever/whoever that
  challenge may be. With heart and backbone
  (compassionate and firm), keep turning your client
  back to face her own challenge.

Coaching from the Middle

Once you have entered into the executive's triangle, there are
some systems lenses you can use to help you stay in the Client
Responsibility Model. The more you understand patterns, homeostasis, boundaries, and the distinct change management roles in a
system, the more you can use them to work from your middle position in the triangle. Then you will be able to help a leader make
choices in the system. You can also watch out for her tendencies
to seek you out as a replacement for the work she needs to be
doing herself.

Patterns in the Leader's System

For the most part we have been using pattern thinking to identify
the dance between you and your client. You can also use it to help
your client address her patterns within her organization. Observe a
high-performing group and contrast it with a floundering one. You
can detect established patterns of interaction within each group that
create and reinforce their results. **You can help your clients learn
to identify the patterns in which they are immersed.**

Following is an example of a powerful pattern co-created by one
of my clients and her team.

· · · · · · ·

Barbara

Barbara was a driving, excellence-oriented executive. However, her
team seemed to be drifting into mediocrity, unable to find a way out.
She spent quite a bit of time worrying about their performance, both

silently and aloud at team meetings. Why couldn't they leave their present plateau of performance? I talked with Barbara and asked about the kinds of interactions she had with her direct reports, both one-on-one and together as a group. I also spoke with each one of the team members and sat in on a meeting. Even though there was a lot of discussion—each person talking both privately and publicly about their desire to excel—there was a central pattern getting in their way.

The "news headline" of the pattern could be described as "Avoid-Avoid." Although Barbara talked about excellence she did not insist on behaviors that would get there. She didn't challenge the actions or inactions of team members leading to their mediocrity. That was her side of the avoiding. The team members avoided challenging each other to higher performance. Neither did they tell Barbara what they needed from her to break through to a higher level. The "Avoid-Avoid" pattern was choking off performance from a talented and well-intentioned team.

. . . .

Addressing a pattern while coaching can get tricky, particularly if you as the coach see it before the other parties do. It is almost always easier for the third person in the triangle to see a pattern better than the two primary players within it. The third person in the middle (in this case, the coach) has just enough distance to get perspective.

So how do I help the leader identify patterns without getting resistance from her when she can't see them? **Asking the leader questions can be useful.** Here are some questions that you can ask your clients to help them identify the patterns around them:[1]

- What does Person A do that seems to trigger Person B's response? What does B do or not do that starts A down that path in the first place?

- Does this interaction have a familiar ring to it? If you were a betting person, could you count on these two people or this group to react in predictable ways?

- Does this recur so often that you could even "Name
  That Tune?" How would this be identified as a news
  headline? For example, it might be "Attack
  Counterattack," or "Bully Finds Placator," or "Rescuer
  Saves the Day," or "Pursuer Chases a Distancer."

In the case of the last example, the pursuer does something to help people retreat. At the same time, those who keep their distance continue to act in a way that brings out the pursuer to chase them. No one is innocent.

Pattern identification needs to be offered respectfully and provisionally. The more tightly you hang on to your way of seeing your client's pattern, the more resistance you are likely to get. An occupational hazard of the middle position is to provide a point of view that receives a lackluster if not hostile reception from the primary parties. There is no objective truth to the *name* you give a pattern. It is only important that the primary players see their circular self-reinforcing dance. Once they acknowledge a familiar tone to their relating, **you can invite them to name the pattern themselves.**

Since patterns are self-reinforcing, they are hard to break, a fact that gets us to the next issue: helping leaders move beyond some of them.

Homeostasis

Homeostasis is a fancy word for the forces keeping the system at its current level of functioning, thus preserving the established patterns. Members of the group may even experience the current level as being highly unstable and chaotic, but there is a sameness to the instability. The group consistently fails to achieve another, more stable plateau. Homeostasis is like a well-functioning thermostat set to a specific temperature that resists change. It has a low tolerance for any variance in temperature.

Neither good nor bad, homeostasis is a natural part of the self-preservation of any system. Organizations, ecological niches, even single-cell amoebas rely on homeostasis for healthy survival. Homeostasis preserves inner stability so that a system can remain at its current level of functioning, which may be very effective. However, homeostasis may cause a system to resist a change that may actually improve its functioning. A system can be too slow in adapting to a change required for its survival.

People in a group can resist change even when they have a sincere desire to change and know intellectually that change would benefit them. These "push back" or "don't change" impulses in a system have undone many a leader. The coach must attend to this natural, nonmalicious resistance in order to help a leader significantly alter a system's way of doing things. Otherwise, an executive's best intentions unravel. Understanding the power of homeostasis is invaluable. It helps both the coach and the leader to take the situation less personally and avoid thinking, "They're doing this to *me*."

At first, it is easy to feel gloomy about systems: "This thing is bigger than all of us!" However, there is a common proverb of systemic thinking: "The unit and focus for change is the system, and the agent of change is the individual." I have found renewed freedom to act within systems when I can identify the predominant patterns and make a choice whether to keep or change my part in them.

The coach's reaction to a client system's homeostasis can get tricky, and the weakness of the Rescue Model comes into full play. Coaches get distracted by a system's "push-back" response and start to believe it is up to them to break through the system's resistance. If, in your middle position between your client and her challenge, you take on your client's job of dealing with her system's homeostasis, you will undertake the mythical job of Sisyphus. He had to roll the rock up the hill, only to see it fall back down, only to roll it back up, then have it slide back down again—repeatedly and forever. In fact, this is one of the chief reasons coaches and consultants burn out. They take sole responsibility for fighting the "push-back" responses in a system.

You serve your clients better when you help *them* deal with the homeostasis of the system rather than taking on the burden yourself. It is essential that you **educate leaders about the natural occurrence of homeostatic resistance to their changes.** Once they see it, it can free them up when they expect a team to "push back." Therefore, **they won't take the resistance personally.** Leaders must be willing, however, to withstand this predictable reaction.

· · · · · · ·

Barbara, continued

Barbara and her team took quite readily to seeing themselves in the pattern of "Avoid-Avoid." They were relieved when they could finally name the dynamic. Then Barbara went after it with a vengeance. In team meetings she recognized the moments when members retreated. She challenged them to do more interdisciplinary work together to reach a high performance level. The team said that they liked it. They had been neglected as a working group, so any attention in that area seemed right to them.

Even though the meetings were much more stimulating, the results did not improve. Actually, Barbara was still dealing with her own internal thermostat—she talked big at the meetings but did not follow through with the challenge one-on-one. The staff lapsed into their old way of doing things when they perceived that Barbara's pressure to change was intermittent.

When we discussed the natural slide to the old pattern that occurred, Barbara was up against a decision point. Was she going to keep the pressure on herself and her team so they could break through to higher results? Yes, she concluded. She pulled it off only because she was vigilant in looking out for the recurrence of the old pattern—in herself and others. She learned that they were not conspiring to resist the change. It was just that the old pattern came so naturally.

· · · · · · ·

When executives raise their internal tolerance for this homeo-static resistance, it serves them well and keeps them out of anxiety triangles for a longer time. **You can help your clients by assist-ing them to anticipate this resistance to change.** It prepares them for the reactions they are likely to get when they change a long-held pattern.

Boundaries

Systems maintain health when they have strong yet permeable boundaries around them. Boundaries that help create a group's iden-tity include rules used by the system: the establishment of who is in and who is out, and the expectations of members' behavior. Sub-groups clarify their roles, finding ways to be open to receiving com-munication and feedback from other parts of the system. Boundaries hold a group together so they do not lose their identity in the crowd (the larger organization). They need to be loose enough, however, to allow information and visitors from other subgroups to flow in and out, enhancing rather than disrupting the group's accomplish-ment of its goals.

Boundaries become invisible to those within the system. Coach-ing from the middle, you can **help leaders see which organizational activities contribute to building healthy boundaries.** Some exam-ples of such activities include the following:

- Developing job expectations

- Enrolling new employees in orientation programs

- Defining what information is confidential and who can know it

- Saying yes to certain projects and no to others

- Clarifying territories of customers and prospects

- Defining protocols

Coaches can help executives review the boundaries of their system. Asking questions for clarity is very useful to leaders. Here are a few:

- Do people know what is expected of them?

- What are the boundaries of this system?

- Are they frequently compromised so that work is difficult to do?

- Are they so rigid that people are not getting essential information from other parts of the organization?

Many ineffective patterns result from the violation of appropriate boundaries. For example, when people are not clear about who has legitimate authority in a system, the pattern of unproductive arguments can derail a project timeline. Constant remaking of the same decisions can significantly slow the manufacture of a product. If members of a system know who has what roles and information, they can operate much more effectively.

• • • • • • •

Barbara, continued

One of the discoveries Barbara made was that the boundaries in her organization would not support the change she wanted. In many places they were too rigid, thus shutting out information from those who needed it.

First of all, the different team members had no habit of sharing information with other team members. Neither did they ask for help across the disciplines. This created too many barriers between them; it was hard to overcome the distance when a need arose for them to "put their heads together" to solve a productivity problem.

Second, Barbara also realized that she was protecting the team too much from the mandates of her boss. In trying to save them from getting anxious about the state of the business, she was lulling them into too low a sense of urgency.

* * * * * * *

Know the Roles That You and Others Play

The previously presented thinking on triangles, patterns, homeostasis, and boundaries has its roots, as I mentioned before, in family systems theory. To link this approach more deeply into the organizational world, I have used the work of Daryl Conner (1993). He applies systems thinking to workplaces undergoing change initiatives. Change initiatives are going on all the time in organizations. Assume that you will deal with leaders who are either on the brink or in the middle of these initiatives. Barbara's case is but one example of such a change.

Conner's research identified four key roles necessary for successful and sustained change efforts in organizations. They are sponsor (and sustaining sponsor), target, advocate, and agent. **Although individuals can play more than one role, it is critical that they are clear about which role they are in at any one time and that they work within the appropriate boundaries of that role.** Often change fails because these roles are not aligned with each other to allow for the maximum opportunity to change the status quo.

These roles are central for executives leading changes in their organization. Coaches need to help the leaders think through these roles carefully. They are simple and obvious in their definition, yet they are hard to enact with integrity because of the ingrained patterns already present in an organization counteracting the change. The coaching role itself is synonymous with the position of change agent from Conner's perspective.

The *sponsor* is the person who has the authority to make a change happen. She legitimizes and sanctions the change (*for example, Susan from the vignette and Barbara, my client*). A sponsor is only a sponsor if she has line authority over the people who will implement the change. She also has control over resources that are needed—for example, money, time, and people. Good sponsors have a clear vision for the change. They identify goals and measurable outcomes for the initiative.

Sustaining sponsors (for example, Tom) are those in the organization who are responsible for sponsoring the change in their own area, a change that may have started with an initiating sponsor higher up in the organization.

Conner defines the **targets** (I prefer *implementers*) as the people "who must actually change" (p. 106). I think of them as the people expected to implement the change (for example, a member in Tom's finance department or a member of Barbara's team). They have direct line responsibilities to the sponsor or sustaining sponsor. They are most effective when they listen, inquire, and clarify their questions and concerns with their sponsor at the beginning of a transition. This way they can commit to the effort rather than falsely complying, and later sabotaging. Their job is to continue to provide information about their experience of the implementation, providing an essential feedback loop in the system.

Excellent implementers can save sponsors from tunnel vision or from being surprised by obstacles that those closest to the change sometimes notice first. Every sustaining sponsor needs first to be an excellent "target" with his own sponsor. The sustaining sponsor should make sure he knows what is expected and commit himself to the change. That way he gets on board with the change goals rather than telegraphing a lack of ownership to the team (as Tom did to his department).

An **advocate** has an idea about how a change can happen, but needs a sponsor for her idea. All change has to be sponsored. An advocate could have any number of reasons for pushing her idea. She may have noticed something in the system that inherently blocks the effectiveness of the implementers, and she wants to improve this situation for them. She may be passionate about the change idea itself. Or she may want something different for herself and her work in the organization. Any of these motivations is legitimate.

Advocates often become frustrated and demoralized when they cannot seem to get anyone to implement their idea. They have left out the key factor, which is to get a sponsor. Savvy advocates promote ideas by showing their compatibility with issues near and dear to sponsors' change projects and goals.

Conner says that a *change agent* actually makes the change. I believe a change agent is the *facilitator* of the change (*for example, Ben*), helping the sponsor and the implementers stay aligned with each other. **To increase your effectiveness as a coach, it is essential to understand the change agent role and its interplay with the other three roles.**

The change agent can work with both the sponsor and the implementers. He can be internal or external to an organization. He can play a number of roles—data gatherer, educator, advisor, meeting facilitator, or coach. He most often has no direct-line authority over the implementers and is therefore in a naturally occurring triangle among sponsor–implementer–agent. Conner believes that this triangle, when the implementers do not report to the agents, is most often doomed to fail. My experience with organizations is more optimistic *if the sponsor retains the role of sponsor and does not abandon the agent to the implementers.* **The goal for a change agent is to use the role in the triangle to help all parties function effectively. That means the sponsor does the tasks of sponsoring, and the implementers do the tasks of accomplishing. The change agent facilitates, without taking on the roles of the other two parties.**

The natural triangle of sponsor–implementer–agent can easily get out of alignment. Since executive coaches are change agents in the middle of this triangle, they must be aware of possible role malfunctions. Sponsors often drop the ball, and implementers sometimes get disconnected from the sponsor and the change effort. When this happens a change agent can often overfunction, filling in gaps left by the sponsor. This is pseudo-sponsoring, à la the Rescue Model, and perpetuates a pattern in the triangle that keeps the system ineffective. The coach can work overtime trying to infuse the sponsor with a sense of urgency or by begging, pleading, threatening, managing, or cajoling the implementers. This sends a warning light that the coach has misaligned his own role in the triangle and that the change effort is in trouble.

It is critical for a coach to work with his client from the perspective of change agent, and work for alignment of these roles within a change initiative. Even though your clients are leaders, the change management role they play with the issue at hand needs assessment and possible alteration. If your client has an issue with her boss, your client is an *implementer* for the moment. Or she may be *advocating* for a change with a peer in another department. Or her boss may expect her to do *change agent* work, which means she has multiple roles and needs to maintain the clarity of each role.

· · · · · · ·

Barbara, continued

Barbara and I reviewed her roles and those of her team. It did not take her long to see that their roles were misaligned. Because she was at a high level in the organization, all of Barbara's direct reports were executives themselves and therefore sustaining sponsors of change initiatives. However, they did not act like sustaining sponsors. They did not grab a hold of change initiatives and sponsor them strongly in their own area. They seemed to leave that up to Barbara. No wonder she was burning herself out.

Barbara discovered another misalignment, now that she understood the roles better. She learned that two of her direct reports were going to her human resources director to find out what Barbara meant in the team meetings! Previously she would have figured their actions saved her time explaining things to them (of course, it also perpetuated the "Avoid-Avoid" pattern). Now Barbara saw that her direct reports were asking the HR director (Barbara's change agent) to fill in for Barbara (which perpetuated an ineffective triangle). Only Barbara could convey the urgency and clarity of her message to the direct reports. She told the human resources director to stop speaking on her behalf, a habit that, though well-intentioned, actually diluted the effort.

• • • • • • •

You can help an executive dramatically increase her effectiveness by helping her enact her change role fully and by assisting her in keeping the boundaries of that role clear from the other roles. You can help the leader clarify what she can expect from others, based on their roles. Just as important, you need to stay within the boundaries of the change agent's role as a coach. **Aiding leaders in defining role boundaries and responsibilities, and keeping them clear, strong, and flexible are some of the most rewarding contributions you as a coach can provide.** It creates a big payoff in organizational change efforts.

The systems perspective of coaching from the middle of the triangle between a leader and her challenge fuels the four phases of coaching outlined in Part Two. I invite you to take the Client Responsibility Model forward with you as you explore the phases outlined in the following chapters. It underlies the reasoning behind the specific actions suggested in each step of the coaching process.

• • • • • • •

CHAPTER FOUR HIGHLIGHTS

The Client Responsibility Model versus the Rescue Model of Coaching

1. Identify and avoid Rescue Model attitudes and behaviors.

2. Use the attitudes and behaviors of the Client Responsibility Model: Sustain a belief in your client's resourcefulness.

3. Support the primary relationship between the leader and her challenge, whatever or whoever that challenge may be. With

heart and backbone (compassionate and firm) keep turning your client back to facing her own challenge.

Patterns in the Leader's System

1. Help the leader identify the patterns in which she is immersed.
2. Ask the leader questions to reveal the central "dance."
3. Offer your identification of the pattern respectfully and provisionally.
4. Invite the client to name the pattern herself.

Homeostasis

1. Help the leader anticipate and prepare for inevitable resistance.
2. Help the leader learn not to take resistance personally.

Boundaries

1. Learn to see organizational activities that promote healthy boundaries.
2. Inquire about the boundary-making activities in the leader's system.

Know the Roles You and Others Play

1. Understand the roles of sponsor, implementer, advocate, and agent.
2. Learn how the triangle of sponsor–implementer–agent can function well or create problems.
3. Help the leader define the boundaries and responsibilities of her role and the roles of those around her for improved alignment.

♦ ♦ ♦ ♦ ♦ ♦ ♦

Part II

. . . .

The Four Phases of Coaching

Phase 1—Contracting

Find a Way to Be a Partner

Those familiar with action research methodology from the organization development field will recognize the four phases of
executive coaching I outline here.[1] They come directly from that
tradition.

The Roots of the Coaching Phases

The five classic phases of action research are (1) entry and
contracting; (2) data collection and feedback; (3) action planning;
(4) implementation and follow through; and (5) evaluation, including either termination of the contract or recycling through the
steps.[2] Action research can take the form of coaching as it does here
in the four phases of coaching in Part Two: contracting, planning,
live-action coaching, and debriefing.[3]

I have combined the action research model with a systems
perspective because each leverages the other for greater results.
Therefore, as I discuss these phases, I highlight areas of systems
assessment and intervention. For example, the systems approach of
noticing and changing patterns actually supports action research
methodology: Action research is based on the belief that intervention in any phase can create change, not just during the implementation step. As soon as an organization begins to engage with

the first phase of action research, the organization can create a heightened self-awareness readying it for change.

In these four phases, I also highlight the issues business coaches need to attend to that are, ironically, underemphasized in the coaching literature. Sometimes coaches avoid them. The issues are focusing on specific business results and dealing with issues of organizational alignment.

Contracting

In many ways, contracting is the most important phase. Both people—coach and leader—build a relationship and establish credibility. The executive wonders, can the coach help me? The coach asks herself, is the executive open to feedback? Together they need to draw the goals and parameters for the coaching relationship and set up expectations that drive the rest of the phases. At this stage, coaches offer clients a taste of what working together will be like.

Contracting can include a new client who solely wants coaching services. Or it may occur with a client who is contracting for a larger organizational intervention. One-on-one coaching with him is only a part of the work that you will do with him and his team. Or coaching may result with an established client for whom you have done a larger project, someone who now wants help in concentrating on his own leadership.

There are a number of important steps for contracting:

- **Joining with the leader**
- **Familiarizing yourself with the leader's challenge**
- **Testing the executive's ability to own his part of the issue**
- **Giving immediate feedback to the leader**
- **Establishing a contract**
- **Encouraging the executive to set measurable goals**

One way to finalize a coaching contract is to start coaching right in the contracting conversation. Then your potential client has a taste of how you work. You can immediately begin a productive partnership and build elements into it that will keep the other phases on track.

Joining with the Leader

There is no getting around good old-fashioned **joining skills** on the front end of contracting—neighborly friendliness and approach-ability, basic humanness, a sense of humor, and sincere interest in the other person. It is the basic ease, flow, and even fun in your conversations that builds strength for the tougher times that will later pull on the fabric of your relationship.

Your client, particularly a new one, needs answers to the following questions. "How quickly can you get on board with me? Do you get what I'm talking about? Are you practical, effective? Do you have some depth to your experience?" He wants to know whether you will really be able to help him. Most often he does not explicitly voice these questions. The executive is doing his own assessment during your first conversations. You have to pass the leader's "smell test."

You need to be conducting your own assessment as well. Executive coaching requires the willingness of the leader to explore his strengths and weaknesses. Wise executives see themselves as not only part of the picture but deeply embedded in the success and disappointments of an organizational effort. When they are willing to look at themselves, energy-draining homeostasis holds less power over the system.

Familiarizing Yourself with the Leader's Challenge

A partnership begins when the leader talks about the specific issue where he is currently stuck. The problem could be with one other person (an employee, boss, or peer) or it could be a work group or larger organizational issue (lack of resources, a visioning effort, downsizing, or work redesign). Often just **listening, following your curiosity about the issue, and constantly restating for clarity** helps the leader in defining the central issue, his opportunities, and challenges.

Use specific listening skills. A whole host of listening skills can enhance the early part of the coaching conversation. I will highlight four here that I use most often at this stage. They come from Robert Carkhuff (1969) and his approach to helping relationships: **concreteness, empathy, confrontation, and respect.**[4]

Concreteness **means inviting the leader to get more specific about his issue.** Executives often speak in global terms and have little patience for details. You are not asking details for details' sake. You are inviting the leader to describe actual behaviors and circumstances so he can see what he really means by his global terms. A lot of leaders articulate global dissatisfaction, but it gets them nowhere. By pushing for specificity, you are doing an enormous favor for the organization, because leaders are often not clear with their staffs about their expectations.

Some questions that elicit a concrete response include the following:

- What specifically frustrates you about the situation?

- Can you give me an example?

- What do you mean?

- When did this happen?

- What specifically do you expect from her?

Empathy is your effort to show you understand the leader's concerns. The more you can express, in your own words, the leader's message, the more he will think, "OK, somebody knows what I'm talking about!" When you are on track with the executive's core concern, you will be addressing his real issue—not the issue you think he means. Following are some examples of using empathy in a coaching conversation:

- "You seem most concerned about the expanding demands of the business and whether you have the staff to cover those demands."

- "Do you mean you are caught between being loyal to the employees who built this company with you and at the same time wanting to take advantage of the hot new stars in the business?"

- "It seems you are struggling with having to give hard feedback to a couple of long-term employees, and they may be oblivious that their performance no longer matches the demands of their positions."

Showing empathy can help a leader sift and weigh his concerns. He can either say, "Yeah, I guess this *is* a big issue for me." Or he can say, "You know, when I hear you put it that way, I'm actually more troubled about something else."

Confrontation does not mean inciting a conflict with the leader. There are plenty of opportunities for real conflict in organizations. In this context, *confrontation* **means pointing out discrepancies between what the leader is saying and what he actually does.** It could be a mismatch between what he said twenty minutes ago to what he is saying now, or between his words and his previous actions. You bring forth the discrepancy in a neutral tone, not with a "gotcha" attitude. You simply hold up a mirror so the leader can make his own judgments about his incongruence.

The more neutral you are about showing the mismatch, the more powerful this intervention can be for the executive. By *neutral* I mean being descriptive about the behavior the leader is doing rather than critical or judgmental. Here are some ways of using confrontation in a coaching conversation:

- "You say excellence is your number one concern, yet you report that you haven't set competitive standards that are up-to-date in your market."

- "In the last ten minutes you have given arguments both *for* creating the new position and *against* it."

- "This is the first time I have heard you question the CEO's direction and lay out a thorough alternative strategy."

Spending time on a leader's discrepancies in behavior can help him finally deal with some contradictions that may have been living in him for months or even years. It helps him get closer to a decision point about them, rather than continually bringing them up to half-consciousness and then ignoring them.

Respect goes beyond holding the executive in high regard or admiring qualities he has. Actually, **it has to do with having a deep belief that he has the capacity and the resources to handle and resolve the situation.** You believe and show that ultimately the leader has the resilience he needs to address his issue. Respect keeps you in the Client Responsibility Model. This is why the Rescue Model is ultimately disrespectful of your client: It takes over his problem-solving accountability. You can use respect in a coaching conversation in these ways:

- "You have successfully dealt with challenges like this before."

- "You actually show more knowledge in this area than you give yourself credit."

- "The combination of traits you bring to the issue— practical savvy along with holding the larger goal in mind—is what the situation calls for."

- "You have a way of using your sense of humor to keep perspective while you wade through the toughest phases of the project."

Once you have engaged the leader by using the four listening skills (concreteness, empathy, confrontation, and respect), he has well articulated his situation. The two of you know more what is at stake, and you share a background from which you will work.

Testing the Executive's Ability to Own His Part of the Issue

When entering a contracting conversation with an executive, I determine whether the leader is willing to explore the possibility that he both enhances and detracts from his own goals. An executive can use coaching as an effective tool only when he is willing to focus on his own functioning. Early on, I test for this necessary condition, since it is not worth making a contract to coach if this willingness is not present.

Right from the beginning, the leader can learn that you do not probe only at the external factors in the situation, but also for the ways in which the leader has contributed to them. The distinguishing characteristic of this kind of coaching is to **keep the executive's habitual response to the issue as the central focus,** *even while the goal is creating a change in the environment.* There are lots of other offers to the leader to find the key outside, for example, a new technique or training. Very few leaders find a coaching partner who helps them develop their own internal resource as the key.

This is not therapy or esoteric wisdom. It is the realization that the leader's greatest leverage for change is his own response to the issue. Your contribution is to assist him in identifying his part of the co-created system. One way to test the leader's willingness to look at his role is to ask questions like these that follow.

If he welcomes this kind of self-reflection, you have a good potential client.

- What recurring patterns are present in this situation?

- Which patterns work well and which detract from the effort?

- How are you a part of these patterns?

- How have you responded to this issue?

- What is your knee-jerk contribution? For example, are you often the overachiever, the blamer, the pursuer, the victim, the helper, the avoider, the parent?

- ⊙ Can you imagine a different pattern?

- How willing are you to develop the stamina required to stop your part of the pattern that is no longer effective?

- How will this help you get to your goal?

- How can I be useful to you?

Giving Immediate Feedback to the Leader

It is at this time that you give your own feedback and observations to the leader. Even if you have just met, you have your own experience of him up to this point. From a systems view, this brief experience gives you a picture of his functioning within the issue. As I discussed in Chapter Two, the use of immediacy is the real gold of any coaching moment. Your own interaction with the executive is a window into his characteristic patterns. Particularly in the contracting phase, it is important to feed back your own experience, here and now, of your client, that is, what is happening between you. Again, you act on the belief that what happens in the immediacy of this moment *is* what happens "out there" in the executive's work world. The feedback needs the characteristics of backbone and heart—frank, specific, not protective, and yet collaborative.

· · · · · · ·

Ned

Ned, a prospective client, called to ask me whether I would do a team-building retreat because there was a lot of dissent among his staff. As we talked and explored the issues, I declined the offer because I thought the one-day event as he wanted to do it would only be a Band-Aid and not really address the issues. He later called to say his staff was going to be doing a survey feedback process instead, and would I submit a proposal? We talked more and, though I believe in the effectiveness of feedback action planning projects, I judged that he had abdicated his authority in the process and that would undercut the effort. I told him as much and said that I would include a coaching contract with him as part of my proposal. At the end of the conversation, he declined my offer but said, "I think I just got some of the best consulting I've ever had, and it was for free."

A month later he called and said he wanted me to coach him. We set up a contracting meeting. He talked about the challenges he faced with his team. And talked. And talked. And talked. I started to have a queasy feeling imagining having to endure his verbose style. I knew I either had to give him my immediate experience and potentially lose him as a client again, or pay for my silence by being a victim of his talking.

I interrupted him after about fifteen minutes, and said, "You know, as I'm listening to you I find it hard to concentrate on what you're saying. I get a breathless feeling, and it's hard to know when I can break in. I also wonder if that's how your staff experiences you."

Ned stopped dead in his tracks and burst out, "That's exactly what I deal with! I'm making so many connections when I'm talking that I lose sight of the conversation." It was in that moment that he knew he would get the real stuff from me, and I knew that he was open and resilient enough to let it in.

· · · · · · ·

Leaders get this kind of immediate feedback so rarely that it gets their attention and tests the cliché they often use but do not live out, "I don't just want another yes-man." I call it the stick-my-finger-in-their-chest moment, which can be delivered at once boldly and respectfully, directly engaging the presence of the client. He may step into the moment, seeking more information and learning about himself. When this happens he will say something to the effect, "This is the kind of feedback I can do something about." Or he might retreat from the frankness, which helps you to decide whether you want to pursue this contract.

A former mentor and coach of mine, John Runyan, called this kind of experience *consumer education*. The idea is to try to find an opportunity early in the contracting phase to use immediacy of feedback with the prospective client. The leader then knows how you coach and whether he wants that kind of coaching. He knows what he is actually buying.

The three necessary conditions for a successful coaching contract are the willingness of the leader to (1) see himself honestly, (2) own his part in the patterns at play, and (3) be receptive to immediate feedback.

For you to say yes or no to the contract depends on whether you have this critical cluster of factors. (Another critical issue, which I will address in Chapter Six, is the leader's ability to look at the sponsor, implementer, advocate, and agent role alignment issues in his organization.)

A Systems View of the Leader's Issue

You can pick up information about the patterns in the system very early in the interaction, such as the possible effect of Ned's speaking style on the team. With systems thinking, you can also wonder about the other side of the pattern. This leader is not overactive in a vacuum; he has help from underinvolved members of the team. To hold a systems view, you must develop emotional neutrality toward the players. There are no pure good guys or bad guys. Everyone is a co-creator.

A word about neutrality: Try as you might to maintain this stance, you can count on being inducted into the system. That is, you will feel the pulls of anxiety the same way the members of the system do. It is not a matter of *if* you get inducted, but *when*.

The utility of being pulled in is that you can learn more about what it is like to be a member of that system. The skill is to recognize this response and find your way back out. For example, as the leader talks about his situation, you need to watch for the emotional pull to take sides between the leader and his team as you listen. The questions you ask the leader to help him identify his part in the web are beneficial to you as well (for example, *What recurring patterns are present in this situation? What is your knee-jerk contribution?*). They remind you that everyone contributes to forming the situation.

The identified problem is usually not the real issue. Difficulties stem from how the client addresses the problem. You need to refrain from the satisfaction of taking sides or deciding on villains, and instead help the system use dormant abilities in all the parties—abilities suppressed by their prevailing responses.

Establishing a Contract

For the external coach, establishing an explicit contract moves the conversation along to specific goal-setting. And for internal change agents in an organization, the explicit offer is equally essential. As an internal organizational coach, I learned that I got into more trouble when I did not make an explicit offer to coach the executive. Without it, I entered into conversations where I was not invited and assumed learning contracts with leaders that I did not have, situations that led to either active resistance or eyes-glazed-over passivity.

Define any requirements you may have in the coaching contract. To the extent that you have expectations essential to the coaching partnership, it pays to mention them up front, rather than trying to bargain or plead for them later. For example, you may want to do any of the following:

- Outline a specific content and sequence of meetings.

- Be present to observe the leader in live action with his team after a specified period of time.

- Have debrief sessions immediately after your client leads key meetings.

These are just a few of the ways to build in mutual responsibility to the contract. For more ideas, see Whitworth, Kimsey-House, and Sandahl (1998).

The offer to coach includes the ability to **describe the options** within the role in a simple way. There are two basic options, which can be combined. The first, occurring the majority of the time, is **behind-the-scenes coaching.** This entails a planning stage (Chapter Six) that helps the manager clarify how he will face a particular situation. There is also a debrief stage (Chapter Eight), when he thinks through how he did, celebrates his success, and plans steps of improvement for the next time.

A second option is what I call **live-action coaching** (Chapter Seven). In this approach, you are present in the room while the leader deals with his issue in real time, whether that entails a meeting with an employee or a group, or a phone call to a coworker. This is a variation on the kind of live-action work that consultants do frequently.

Encouraging the Executive to Set Measurable Goals

Once you and the leader have settled on a coaching contract, you need to clarify **goals for the contract.** This involves the traditional consultation process of setting specific goals and outcomes. Because executive coaching involves working with executives on their own leadership issues and because many of the issues revolve around how they work with others, less experienced coaches can let actual business results get lost in the process.

By the time a coach arrives on the scene, a leader may have been mired in a problem for a long time. Sometimes he and his team start focusing only on the interpersonal issues or personality traits of each other and lose sight of the business issues. New coaches can get distracted by the leader's focus on himself and lack of attention to measurable results. Out of desperation the leader may say, "I need to get along with my team better," or "I need to be more patient," or "I need an open door policy." All of the things the leader says he needs to do differently may be true—or may not be true. It depends on what he wants to accomplish, what is not working, and why.

Focusing on specific outcomes is essential. How will the organization benefit if the leader becomes more collaborative, more approachable, more decisive, or clearer? That these changes would help productivity in the organization may seem obvious at the time. However, by helping the leader articulate the actual business changes he wants, you assist him. In some ways, becoming more collaborative, more approachable, more decisive, or clearer are the leader's personal goals for achieving specific business goals. It is important that executive coaches not confuse personal goals with the business outcomes, because clients do it all the time.

There are, therefore, two kinds of goals the executive needs to work on: **business goals**—getting external results; and **personal goals**—what the leader has to do differently in how he conducts himself in order to get the business results. The leader's personal goals, the challenges he faces in pulling off the business goals, *must follow* the external business goals. For example, say he wants to improve his listening skills. He needs to know for what purpose and for what value to the organization. Granted, better listening makes the leader a better human being, but what is the "so what" value for the organization? The executive gains—and you gain—much more credibility when he links his personal goals to business achievements.

Having an outcome focus can make the difference between the leader continuing or giving up when he hits daunting obstacles. Executives have told me they are afraid they will feel self-indulgent to be "merely" developing themselves with a coach. It is not self-indulgent, it is essential to the business. Get them to say how. Also, linking the coaching effort to a business result will highlight and prioritize the business areas that need attention.

Robert Crosby (1998) has a useful and straightforward description of business goals and their measures. He organizes goals into three arenas: (1) **bottom-line,** (2) **work-process,** and (3) **human relations goals.** For productivity to increase, all three areas need to be addressed. **Bottom-line goals** are the reason the organization exists, to produce products, revenue numbers, or services. **Work-process goals** address *how* the work is accomplished, from the beginning to the end of procedures, projects, and processes, in order to achieve the bottom-line goals. **Human relations goals** focus on how people collaborate to accomplish both the bottom-line and the work-process goals.

Measures need to be established for these outcomes that are as behaviorally specific as possible and relevant to the goal itself. As a coach, you need to strongly encourage the leader to identify a measure for each business goal.

Examples of goals and their measures are listed in Table 5–1.

Another resource for goal-setting with clients is Hargrove (1995). He discusses the use of breakthrough thinking to achieve stretch goals.

It is important that your client keeps the ownership for deciding which goals and measures to pursue. You cannot have more investment in them than the leader. It is your job to work hard helping him be specific about his goals. It is his job to work hard ensuring that they are the right goals for the business.

Table 5.1. Business Goals and Measures.

Arena of Goal	Goal Category	Measure of Goal Outcome
Bottom-Line (Why the organization exists)	Revenue	$10 million increase in revenue
	Profit	15 percent increase in profit
	Budget	Meet budget
	Market share	10 percent increase in market share
	Quantity of production or customers	20 percent higher production levels, 30 percent more customers
Work Process (How the work gets accomplished, from input to throughout to output)	Timeframes for projects	50 percent reduction in project timeframe
	Quality levels of product	80 percent reduction in product defects
	Quality levels of service	Placement in the top 10 percent of national customer satisfaction index
	Cost reduction	30 percent reduction in employee turnover
Human Relations (How people collaborate to accomplish the work)	Clarified decision-making process and alignment of roles	95 percent adherence to the decision and role matrix established at beginning of project
	Improved conflict management practices	80 percent reduction in grievances filed
	Wider participation of work groups	Work teams have decision authority over 50 percent of their work three months after training in team self-sufficiency

Therefore, it is the coach's responsibility to ensure that the goal-setting conversation is sequenced for best results, starting with the business issue and segueing to the leader's personal challenge to achieve results.

- Encourage the leader to name the *business results* needed.

- Find out what *team behaviors* need to be different to accomplish the results.

- Explore what *personal leadership challenges* the executive faces in improving these results and team behaviors.

- Identify *specific behaviors the leader needs to enhance* or change in himself.

The sequence links business results with team behaviors and with behavior changes in the executive. The connection builds between those three areas in the leader's awareness so he knows what to attend to and where to look for gaps. Throughout the coaching process, you can inquire about all three: the business results, the team's actions, and the leader's changes. Building these links into your conversations increases his understanding of the connections, shows him how indispensable it is to keep the three areas together, and points out how valuable your interventions are to his effort.

Let's go back to the executive, Barbara, and see how goals can be built from her presenting issue. She wanted excellence but was getting mediocrity from a team that was fragmented in their efforts by an avoid-avoid pattern and a lack of strong sustaining sponsorship among her direct reports. This conversation is long because it takes a great deal of exploration to keep the three variables in play and interrelating.

. . . .

Barbara

COACH: You'll get farther and know when you have arrived if you set more explicit goals for the business, your team, and yourself.

BARBARA: I've got goals. I want us to be the best game in town! Number one in the company.

COACH: But what does that mean—in what area and at what level? If you say, "Jump," how is your team going to know how high?

BARBARA: Well, it's all about market share this year. We need to increase market share by 4 points (*bottom line goal and measure*).

COACH: And as you have been learning about what works and doesn't work on this team, what do your direct reports—the vice presidents—have to do to make this goal more achievable?

BARBARA: Well, it's ridiculous that all the vice presidents don't have the same information on the key issues that have an impact on market share. They're still operating out of their silos and not thinking strategically about what in their area should be known by all (*work process issue*).

COACH: I see how critical that is, but how would you know if what they changed made a difference? If they just sent reports to each other, it doesn't mean they'll read them or use them strategically to increase market share.

BARBARA: I see what you mean. We could dream up processes for information flow and still get nowhere. Wait a minute. Maybe the problem is what we cover in our meetings and how the whole meeting is run. Actually, I may be perpetuating the problem with the kind of meeting it is. I'm going to charge them with restructuring our meetings to meet the information and design needs of the business (*work process goal*).

COACH: Great. Now think about them working well. What would be happening if your VPs got out of their silos more and were better informed? And especially think of what they would be doing that would help increase the share by four points.

BARBARA: For one thing, we need to shorten our response time by a week between getting the latest sales figures and tweaking our sales tactics (*work process measure*).

COACH: OK—that's a start. As you continue to work on this, you may discover even deeper work process issues. You also need to define your expectations of team behaviors, how individuals need to act differently to turn this whole thing around.

BARBARA: Yeah, they need to step up more and deliver world-class performance.

COACH: And by "stepping up" you mean . . . ?

BARBARA: Do I have to spell everything out? These are vice presidents for goodness sake! By now they should know what it means.

COACH: If that were the case, Barbara, you wouldn't be in the situation you're in and we wouldn't be having this conversation. You have really bright people reporting to you. But they've been pulled in so many directions lately, they have lost focus.

BARBARA: So, what are you saying, I have to tell them how to be a team player? Isn't that insulting? I hate cheerleading senior people. It's demeaning.

COACH: I'm not talking about cheerleading or talking down to people. I'm talking about setting expectations that get everybody focused on key team behaviors that make a competitive difference. We're talking about "soft skills," but it takes hard-headed business people to be explicit about them. When you think of your meetings, what about them would you say doesn't show world-class behavior?

BARBARA: Lackadaisical commitment. They say they're on board, but then they don't drive their managing to get the results.

COACH: You're talking about their sponsorship. You're not going anywhere without higher commitment from them (*human relations goal—expectations of team behaviors*).

BARBARA: How am I going to get that?

COACH: Exactly—how are you going to get it? Now you're talking about what you are going to have to do differently to have more committed VPs as sustaining sponsors. What more could you be doing (*necessary change in leader behavior*)?

BARBARA: Well, for one thing, I could talk more about the pressure I'm getting from my boss about market share. And I could be more active about talking to each one about their commitment, too—especially their concerns. I know I'm not getting all of the real stuff.

COACH: That would be great, because if you get the real stuff, you'll probably learn more about what they need to get more committed.

By the way, what would be a measure of stronger sponsorship on their part?

BARBARA: They would stop going to the HR director to find out what I want. And they would be commenting on the key issues, giving their best thinking, whether it directly affected their own area or not. Then I would know they were informed and up-to-date. They would proactively be coming to me with ideas on how they're going to close the gap on share that would include coordinating with other departments (*human relations goal—team behavior measures*).

COACH: If that's how you're going to measure it, you're going to have to track it, be aware of when it's happening and when it's not, and whether you're doing what you said you needed to do to get there as well.

BARBARA: I think if we improved our decision making (*human relations goal—team behavior expectation*) we'd get there faster, too.

COACH: Now you're on a roll. What's the problem?

BARBARA: In meetings, the decision making is pathetic. It takes forever, people don't remember what decisions were made, and so they have to get remade.

COACH: You run those meetings, Barbara. What do you need to do to improve that (*necessary change in leader behavior*)?

BARBARA: If I knew I'd be doing it.

COACH: Often, leaders don't tell people the kind of decision they are making, for example, is the decision going to be consultative to the leader or consensual by everyone? Team members don't know how to be productive in the conversation. That's one thing you could do right away to make a change—be more explicit about which kind of decision you're making (*human relations measure*).

BARBARA: I could do that. I don't tell people the decision style I'm using. You're right—that could be confusing.

COACH: If you go in that direction, what do you want from them?

BARBARA: I want them to give their input on decisions. I want to hear their reservations, and I want to hear alternative solutions. And I want everyone to remember what the decision was and follow through with their part of it (*human relations—team behavior measures*).

COACH: You've just named the measures for this one. What would be the easiest way to know you and your team were on or off track?

BARBARA: It would be easy enough for me to facilitate a summary coming from them at the end of each meeting about what decisions were made and the kind of decision it was. That way I could test against their understanding just how clear I was with announcing the style of decision up front and whether I stayed faithful to it. I could also scan to see whether I got sufficient participation and commitment from all the VPs.

COACH: To the extent that you tell them right then whether you got it or not, you will be combining measuring your progress with giving immediate feedback, which can be a powerful tool toward improving bottom-line results.

• • • • • • •

These conversations are arduous but worth the investment the executive and coach put into them. Barbara was able to identify goals and measures in each of the areas—bottom line, work process, and human relations. She made a connection between raising market share and increasing the quality of her business meetings. What is more, she knows her obligation to be clearer about the decision-making process in those meetings.

Some of the measures in the conversation with Barbara identify successful progress toward human relations goals. These are always the toughest to measure. The point of identifying measures for them is to provide a way for executives and their teams to know whether they are making progress toward those goals.

The ultimate measure is whether they make their bottom-line goal. But it is the team behaviors and work processes that will get them there. The measures for these goals provide the leader and the team with growing knowledge of the specific actions that directly affect business outcomes. They will be more likely to commit to change their habitual actions when they see that new individual and team behaviors directly affect results.

Slow Down Goal-Setting to Speed Up the Action Later

Clients are often impatient to "get on with it" during the contracting phase. Once they feel confident that they can work with a coach, they want to start the action. However, without clear goals and measures for those goals, neither leader nor coach is focused enough to choose the most effective course of action. Leaders are often impatient and irritated with thorough goal conversations. They act as though the time it takes is a real problem for them. I used to think, "They're busy executives. Maybe they're right. I'm being too picky."

What is really happening? The leader is drawing a blank on getting more specific and more rigorous about his goals. He then lashes out with impatience at the process. It is too uncomfortable to experience the void in the conversation that stems from the leader's lack of clarity at the time. He would rather pop out of his discomfort and head for the action. He has been living, as have most people in modern organizations, in a fire-ready-aim mode. It is astonishing how often leaders ignore the goal-setting process. I have come to the conclusion that this task—like many that involve people processes with hard-line results—is simple, but not easy. Goals are simple and obvious to understand, but difficult to pull off well and consistently.

Though it may seem like swimming against the current, you need to slow the executive down long enough to establish clear goals, so he can be productive during the implementation. With no clear guidelines, the action phase of a change effort slows down because of hurried, misdirected efforts. You need to keep the client from bullying you out of a clear goal-setting process. You must bring backbone and confidence to your conviction that there is efficiency in doing it. If you have to, be a broken record about your conviction.

A leaders' crankiness with you when you persist in a conversation that seeks specific goals and outcomes has very little to do with your effectiveness. It has more to do with his own reactions to doing the hard work of aiming himself and the organization, of honing in on specifics. Stay with him and keep inquiring about goals. You will get a reputation for being a hard-nosed business person—not a bad rap!

Now, there is no reason to be Attila the Hun about this. Sometimes a business situation is too ambiguous to be able to clarify what work process or human relations goals would support achieving the bottom-line result. A way to proceed is to encourage the leader to establish, as best as he can, work process and human relations goals that begin to aim at the bottom-line result. Then he can establish midpoint checks of the measures to calibrate them and see whether they take him and his team in the right direction. The specifics set at the beginning can be adjusted later if needed, but spend the energy up front to set them, and monitor them as the leader proceeds with the action.

When the executive connects improvements in his leading to specific work goals, he also builds in his own biofeedback system.

He realizes how his own efforts have helped or hindered goal achievement, how he can sustain success. This kind of emphasis on goals can also give leaders incentive to become more specific with projects beyond those discussed with their coach.

* * * * * * *

CHAPTER FIVE HIGHLIGHTS

Join with the Leader

1. Begin building a foundation for the relationship.

2. Engage in mutual assessment of the fit for a working partnership.

Familiarize Yourself with the Leader's Challenge

1. Listen. Follow your natural curiosity.

2. Empathize. Show you understand the client's core concerns.

3. Confront discrepancies. Help the leader notice inconsistency in thought and action.

4. Show respect by demonstrating your belief in the leader's capabilities.

Test the Executive's Ability to Own His Part of the Issue

1. Keep the leader's response to his challenge as the central issue.

2. Test the leader's willingness to reflect on his part of the issue.

Give Immediate Feedback to the Leader

1. Feed back your here and now experience of the leader.

2. Make your feedback relevant to the leader's business issue.

Establish a Contract

1. Make the coaching offer explicit.

2. Describe the options.

   • Behind the scenes planning and debrief
   • Live-action intervening

Encourage the Executive to Set Measurable Goals

1. Sequence the leader's business and personal goal setting.

   - Encourage the leader to name the *business results* needed.
   - Find out what *team behaviors* need to be different to accomplish the results.
   - Explore what *personal leadership challenges* the executive faces in improving these results and team behaviors.
   - Identify *specific behaviors the leader needs to enhance* or change in himself.

2. Help the leader identify bottom-line, work-process, and human relations goals and measures.

3. Continually link business results to team behaviors and to the leader's changes in his own leading.

4. Slow down during the goal setting in order to speed up the action later.

◆ ◆ ◆ ◆ ◆ ◆ ◆

6

· ·

Phase 2—Action Planning
Keep Ownership with the Client

Coaching goes beyond a venting session and accomplishes more than a simple increase in the leader's understanding of her dilemma. To help your client get to the action, you can work with her through these steps of the planning phase:

1. **Move the executive from general venting to a specific plan.**
2. **Help the leader identify her side of the pattern in the situation.**
3. **Address issues of organizational and role alignment.**
4. **Plan for resistance to the executive's actions.**
5. **Determine whether you as the coach have a live-action coaching role during the leader's implementation of her plan.**

I will begin by exploring the importance of Step 1. Steps 2, 3, and 4 have been covered extensively in earlier chapters. In this chapter, I will concentrate on how they play out in the planning phase. Step 5 helps you to decide the next piece of work in your coaching role with the client.

Move the Executive to Specifics

Once the issues surface and your client has chosen goals, you can help her identify an action plan and focus the leader on her immediate next step. Getting from dilemma, to goal, to action can be difficult while immersed in an issue. The leader may bog down in a variety of ways: resist making specific plans, experience conflicting loyalties, remain entangled in her anger at a subordinate, or fear a conflict. In addition, she may feel overwhelmed by the tasks that need to get done.

Some executives feel so relieved to get their problems off their chest that they do not move to the next step. Their stress may be temporarily lowered just by having a conversation about the situation. Since they feel better (even though it is temporary), they act as though the problem has improved. It has not. A coach does the leader no favors in ignoring her lack of directed action. Without a plan, the leader will return to the situation and repeat the same responses.

For example, I was in coaching conversations with Rich, a CEO, who had this tendency to "stay in the talk." As he spoke about his issue, it became clear that he had a handle on it. He knew the key aggravators, and he knew his "game"—how he contributed to it. He enjoyed discussing the causes of the difficulty and even had good ideas of what the situation needed. But he was unwilling to focus on the uphill climb it took to *change* the circumstances. He never got to a plan and the problem was never solved.

To avoid this inaction you need to encourage the leader to **identify a specific next step.** You do this by exploring the five-step planning road map (presented at the beginning of this chapter) with your client. In terms of Step 1—helping the leader choose a specific plan of action—sometimes a leader can identify a specific step immediately. Other times, a leader's next step will emerge from reviewing the other four tasks first.

Help the Leader Identify Her Side of the Pattern

Leaders often think that planning strategies means figuring out what to tell others to do, and therefore they focus on how others need to change. Although this outward direction may be required, the leader must not leave out the ways she has been a critical factor in the situation. The leader's path to her own reactivity needs special attention. Does she plead, insist, and cajole; stonewall, deflect, and defend; or become philosophical and continuously entertain ideas while not committing to action? The plan should **focus on the actions of the leader**—what does *she* need to do to change *her* behavior?

The following example shows a leader's discovery of her pattern of interaction.

• • • • • • •

Miriam

Miriam was the director of a division with ten departments under her. She had one manager, Sam, who was constantly under-performing—missing deadlines, not dealing with employee issues, and fighting fires rather than preventing them. Miriam was fed up with him, yet Sam had a real flair for the actual performance of the service that his department delivered. Customers loved him.

Miriam and I talked about the many issues she needed to address with Sam, and which ones to tackle first. I asked the usual questions about her previous discussions with Sam. Are you specific about the issues and your expectations? Do you ensure Sam understands what you require? Do you give deadlines?

Then we explored how these conversations usually go and Miriam's part in them. She first talked about Sam's unresponsiveness. "His passivity when I talk to him drives me crazy! He's a professional—why doesn't he think for himself? He never anticipates beyond this week's demands. Do I have to do all his thinking for him?"

"Miriam," I said, "that's not exactly focusing on what you do. That's all about Sam. I know it's hard to get him out of your line of sight, but don't let him take over your thinking! What's your part in this dance?"

When Miriam was able to talk about her side of their discussions, it became apparent that she had fallen into her dominant pattern. She often engaged in "selling" to Sam—what was good for his career, how a different management style was going to benefit him, how great the department would be if he held a vision of excellence for his employees, and on and on.

The pattern between them was one of overenthusiastic salesperson (Miriam) and indifferent prospective buyer (Sam). His indifference was intolerable to Miriam, which led her to escalate her sales style, which further entrenched Sam. Every time she went into her selling mode, Sam became more reluctant and more likely just to give lip service to her ideas. When Miriam realized that, in fact, she knew very little what Sam actually thought about any of these initiatives, she became even more angry.

We focused on Miriam's side of the selling dance as part of action planning, and discussed how to alter the conversation by changing her side of the pattern. The critical ingredient was her response in the situation, more than the content of the conversation or Sam's response.

· · · · · · ·

This was a classic cycle of a two-sided, self-reinforcing pattern. Miriam's reaction fostered Sam's underfunctioning response, and her behavior undermined the very thing she wanted. Sam's action seemed to jump-start, not him to action, but Miriam to overaction—and more of the same in a ceaseless, mindless circle.

Miriam was so locked into this style that she lost sight of her goals in the discussions. Since she usually sold ideas successfully, this lost sale knocked her off balance. Their conversations usually ended with Sam minimally voicing compliance and Miriam feeling uneasy about any real prospect for change.

It can be very useful to the leader to help her identify these patterns for herself. Invite her to notice her internal reaction when she gets into a repetitive pattern. If she is prepared to recognize her experience, she may then discover the pattern and the triggers to it. Any of a number of internal states can signal an automatic pattern:

- Exhibiting indecisiveness or lack of direction

- Experiencing frustration that has no apparent resolution

- Self-blaming

- Feeling closed-minded to another's input

- Lashing out at someone else

- Increasing activity to a frantic pace

In Miriam's case, the internal signal was her high frustration level and her negative judgments about Sam's "passivity" and "unprofessionalism."

When a client is so frustrated that she can only focus on what the other person is doing wrong, it is a sign that she is truly stuck in *her own side* of the pattern. This is an example of *internal* homeostasis that will keep Miriam from doing anything differently. She needs to develop the ability to step back, get some distance, and be able to see both sides in a more neutral way, including her own contribution to a pattern that no longer works. Only then will she gain some freedom to think creatively about how she might change her side.

During the planning phase of coaching, Miriam identified the pattern with Sam, the overselling and reluctant buying. She could even see some humor in the knee-jerk, fits-like-a-glove nature of it, her impulse to oversell to reluctant buyers. She wondered why she had not seen this before.

Address Organizational and Role Alignment Issues

A leader does not manage in a vacuum. The executive will not be successful if she only focuses on her own personal challenges as a leader. The change management roles (sponsor, implementer, agent, and advocate) need attention. As the coach, you assist the leader by **addressing key organizational factors to ensure that your client's plan is appropriately aligned.** Some of these factors include sponsorship and authority in the system, decision-making processes, and clarification of the sponsor–implementer–advocate–agent roles and responsibilities within cross-functional work groups.

A leader's plan needs to involve the most effective level of intervention. Ask basic questions: Is the leader dealing with the right issue? Is she going to talk to the right person? In order to answer these questions, **you as coach can ask about areas that help organize the leader's action plan, questions that get at some of the most typically ambiguous or misaligned factors in an organization.** A leader needs to clarify these areas before she can act effectively:

- In the presenting issue, who is the sponsor? The implementers? The agent? What role is your client playing?

- Can the executive initiate and sponsor her own action, or does she need sponsorship from someone else? (Answering this question can completely shift the focus of the coaching, and therefore the plan, to a more powerful arena.)

- Who has decision-making authority on this issue? Is the leader the decision maker?

- If so, has she decided which decisions she will make and which she will delegate?

- How does she want to increase participation within the work group?

- Are the groups related to the issue clear about their roles? Do they know to whom they are accountable and for which items? What is the leader's responsibility to these groups?

- Has the leader communicated these factors to the people who need to know?

The above questions bring more rigor to the planning process. By inviting the leader to address issues of organizational and role alignment thoroughly, you can help her leverage her plan to greater success. Here is how organizational and role alignment issues played out in Miriam's case.

· · · · · · ·

Miriam and Alignment

When Miriam and I discussed organizational factors, it became clear why Sam never changed his approach to his department. A peer of Miriam's, Ross, constantly pulled Sam off his duties so Sam could resolve Ross's last minute customer service issues. Sam came out smelling like a rose. On top of that, Miriam and Ross's boss, Jim, the executive vice president, congratulated Sam for these heroic efforts. Miriam wanted Sam to do more advanced planning work so the heroic efforts would be unnecessary (they drove labor costs up, for which Jim gave Miriam a hard time). But no one puts on ticker-tape parades for "heroic" planning. Miriam's selling style was actually a tacit pleading with Sam to ignore the executive vice president's kudos, which of course he would not do.

Miriam would continually be defeated in her efforts with Sam as long as this larger organizational pattern involving her sponsor and peer remained unaddressed. She decided she needed first to talk with Jim to make sure her efforts to resolve these issues aligned with his goals. Miriam said, "I can't believe I didn't see this before. Jim's undoing all my efforts to change Sam's management style. I've got to tell him."

"And what are you going to tell him?" I asked.

She said, "That he's screwing up my development plans for my division! He says he supports me, then he goes and does this!"

I said, "Miriam, that and a dollar-fifty will get you a cup of coffee. Barging into Jim's office with your disappointment will probably not change the system."

"What do you mean?" she asked.

"This is going to be a huge change for everyone, including Jim," I answered. "You've got to address this issue in a way that links it to something Jim holds near and dear to his heart. Otherwise, there's not enough incentive for him to change. It's too much work for too little payoff. How could Jim benefit?"

She said, "Labor costs! He's always getting on me for my labor costs. And the biggest spikes in labor happen in Sam's department. That's what's in it for him."

Miriam had her conversation with Jim and linked what she wanted to accomplish to Jim's goals around labor. Rather than merely selling him on the connection, however, she needed to genuinely inquire about whether he saw a significant connection to his goals. When he agreed that he did, she told him of the dilemma that his support of Sam's (and ultimately Ross's) fire fighting had on her goals. It was not until Jim was willing to support Miriam's standards for Sam that this issue had any chance of resolution.

· · · · · · · ·

In Miriam's planning stage, she discovered that she needed to talk with Jim first. Assessing alignment issues has the potential of leveraging a leader's plan to higher effectiveness. The executive studies the context surrounding her issue for factors that have an impact on it.

Part of assessing the context means looking at areas of resistance to any proposed change. Remember, resistance can merely mean the forces that operate to keep things in place.

Plan for Resistance to the Executive's Actions

Some good old-fashioned skepticism can sometimes be useful. What's to say that the leader's plan will work? There is a reason the leader wants coaching on the issue. If it were as simple as fitting alignment pieces of a puzzle together, the executive probably would have moved beyond her dilemma on her own by now. A coach can discuss with the executive the powerful forces in place that will push back on the leader, even as the executive moves toward ensuring a more functional alignment of the issues. The move in the system toward homeostasis—keeping the current balance of forces stable—is powerful, nonrational, and often unconscious or unacknowledged (see Part One). Even when Miriam receives Jim's sponsorship for her plan with Sam, she does not get a guarantee of success when she puts her plan with Sam into action.

Leaders need to **plan for the inevitable resistance** they will experience in executing their plan. Sometimes executives enter into a coaching process enthusiastic about their plan but unprepared for the resistance. Afterward they might say, "Well, *that* was a lousy idea; it didn't work out." Instead of having them unrealistically optimistic, you as coach can invite them to think about what they are going to do precisely *when their plan does not work*. After all, that is the real challenge, when they have to bring themselves fully to the moment.

Managing resistance can help leaders develop a realistic determination regarding their plan rather than an ungrounded optimism. It can build their capacity to remain in sticky situations that activate anxiety. They may not be so easily thrown off course when they experience the inevitable static in the system.

There is power in imagining a successful situation beforehand and rehearsing for its outcome. There is also power in imagining what to do about the resistance that might derail a project. Both preparations are ways of planning for success. **It can be highly productive to encourage your clients to imagine the resistance that could sink their initiatives. This includes their *internal* resistance as well.** It is not a pleasant experience. But with some thought put into pinpointing their individual triggers, you can help executives increase their chance for pushing through the resistance.

For example, a leader may know that, without fail, she backs off from her plan when three particular people come up with reasons against it. She can then *choose* to keep moving ahead, even if those three people do their predictable side of the dance. It also helps to identify the judgments she thinks people will have when she persists. "Well, they'll think I'm being unreasonable, unreliable. They may even complain to my boss."

You can have the executive imagine beyond the impasse. Ask her what she will do to stay on course. You may go through many repetitions of, "Then what will you do?" You are helping her build tolerance for her own discomfort at facing the resistance to her new pattern. When she fully explores these scenarios, it can sometimes be freeing, even funny. She can see how transparent everyone's resistance can be when she has pictured herself withstanding it, making it possible to last long enough to get to the other side. In Miriam's case, planning for resistance helped her prepare for the change she wanted.

* * * * * * *

Miriam Plans for Resistance

When I first asked Miriam what different interactions she wanted from Sam, her response was, "I am so frustrated by his lack of vision that I can't describe what having it would be like." Finally she came up with a description. "He would be proactively coming to me with ideas about how to enhance the department."

* * * * * * *

Sometimes an interim step is to challenge the client to get behaviorally specific about her expectations of the other person (*"He would be proactively coming to me with ideas"*). This opens a crack in the door, often relaxing her commitment to an old way of thinking about the other person, thus giving her a breathing space to get creative about her own side of the dance.

• • • • • • •

We had discussed what Miriam could do differently in her pattern with Sam. She could do less of the talking and Sam could do more. That would both decrease her selling and increase his proactivity.

"But, Miriam," I said. This is not going to be easy street. You and Sam have been operating like this for years. You could do the old pattern in your sleep. You *and* he are going to do and say things in the conversation that will keep the 'strong selling–no buying' dance locked into place. What will he do to keep it going?"

Miriam knew that answer. "Get a blank look on his face and slouch in his chair. That drives me crazy."

"Actually, it drives you to stronger selling," I said. "What will you do to keep the old pattern going?"

Miriam said, "I can't stand his sullen silences. Five seconds of pause in the conversation is all I can take. Then I'm off again."

"So what are you going to do differently?" I asked.

She said, "We'll have a give-and-take discussion, and I won't take it over."

"Sounds great," I said. "Then what are you going to do when you're on your second round of selling because you've just blown past the pauses in the conversation?"

Miriam got a blank look on her face. "What do you mean?"

"Well," I said. "You know it's going to happen. This conversation isn't going to be perfect the first time out. You have to give yourself a break. Rely on getting stuck in the old stuff, and be willing to do something different when you notice it. Here's an example. No matter where you are in the conversation, when you notice you've gone on automatic, stop and ask Sam a question. And don't say a word until after he answers it, even if that's longer than five seconds, even *way* longer than five seconds."

"Oh," she said, reflecting on how the conversations usually go. "Yeah, that would be different."

• • • • • • •

As you can see in this conversation, the leader thinks of a different action to take and anticipates the push-back response from the other person. She imagines both falling back into her old pattern, and then moving beyond it to a distinctly different response that keeps her on track with her plan.

Determine Whether You Have a Live-Action Coaching Role

The coaching contract can extend beyond behind-the-scenes planning with the leader. An executive coach can actually be present in real time when the leader puts her plan into play. This is what I call *live-action* coaching. We will explore it much more in depth in Chapter Seven. Essentially, live-action coaching means that the coach is with the executive while she is "on the job." The coach can directly observe how the leader executes her plan and what strengths and challenges she has in implementing it. The coach can also intervene in the moment to help keep the executive on track. It is a powerful coaching tool and one that needs to be carefully contracted for in the planning session to be most successful.

Under what circumstances would a coach suggest live-action coaching to an executive? There are three criteria to keep in mind when considering live-action coaching:

- The level of trust built up between the coach and the executive—the higher the trust the more likely live-action coaching will be successful.

- The degree to which the leader fails to see and self-correct her pattern when she is in the middle of it— live-action coaching is a tool for a leader's pattern change.

- The extent to which you need calibration of the behind-the-scenes coaching—you may want to

observe the degree of shift in the leader's behavior
and the team's reactions as well.

Level of Trust

The executive has to trust the coach to bring the coach directly into
her live work setting. The trust entails two key elements: (1) the
coach will not overstep his boundaries in the executive's work life,
and (2) the coach will not confront the executive with an ego-
damaging challenge in front of her employees. This is tricky business
because a live-action coach can very effectively challenge the leader
in front of others in a way that can be extremely useful to and wel-
comed by the leader. The executive needs to know that the coach is
acting respectfully when he challenges her, and that he will not suddenly become a pseudo-supervisor to the executive's employees.

Because of these fine lines, live-action coaching usually follows
an already established executive–coach relationship, one that works
effectively for some time. I do live-action coaching either when
executives have been long-term clients, or when they have experienced me in extensive contracting and planning phases during
which they have shown their capacity to receive feedback and learn
from it. Both the coach and the executive have walked enough
down the path of immediacy and feedback to ante up to live-action
coaching.

Tool for Pattern Change

Live-action coaching can be very useful when leaders get stuck in
their patterns and cannot get out of ineffective routine behaviors
with their team. Live-action intervening helps the executive experience kinesthetically the opportune times for changing a pattern.
The coach can stop a leader midstream and suggest an alternative
action. The in-the-moment self-correction of the executive can
help her notice and then anticipate those times when she goes on
automatic. Live-action intervening can speed up the change process
as well, when combined with behind-the-scenes coaching.

Opportunity to Observe

I suggest finding a time in all coaching contracts to observe the executive. At some point, I want to see the executive in action, not only to hear her story of her actions. I then get a fuller sense of the reinforcing patterns that others contribute to the dance as well as those that complement the leader's side of the dance.

Define the Live-Action Role

Rigor is required for live-action coaching. **The role of the coach needs to be clearly defined beforehand.** A range of options is available (see Figure 6.1) and needs to be discussed and agreed upon. Otherwise, the leader may feel blindsided or abandoned during the session due to a mismatch of expectations.

At one end of the spectrum, the least active option, is the observer. As coach you benefit from seeing the executive in action. You receive information beyond the leader's telling of the experience. However, if I am in the room, I prefer to offer as much feedback as possible, and observing provides the lowest influence of the live-action coaching options.

The other end of the spectrum is the "stop action" option. You contract with the leader that you may call a time-out at any time and debrief with her about what she is doing, right on the spot. This highest impact option also requires the most trust between executive and coach. The leader has to be comfortable with the possibility that she could be debriefing her weaker skills in front of other people. Leaders with confidence in themselves as learners—and who

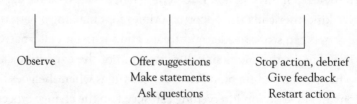

Observe	Offer suggestions	Stop action, debrief
	Make statements	Give feedback
	Ask questions	Restart action

Figure 6.1. Live-Action Coaching Interventions.

have a sense of humor about their own foibles—are the best candidates for this option. A middle-ground option is to offer the executive suggestions or questions during the action that do not interrupt the flow of the action. When done well, the leader continues with her train of thought, either utilizing or ignoring the coach's suggestions, depending on whether the leader can incorporate the suggestion in the moment.

The following example shows planning for live-action coaching with Miriam.

• • • • • • •

Miriam Plans for Live Action

I told Miriam I could sit in on her next session with Sam. "It's one sure way that will help you notice when you get into your selling pattern," I said.

"How would it work?" she asked.

"You would have your conversation with Sam," I told her. "I can coach you right in the moment to enhance your managing. I won't do your work for you or take over the conversation. It will be more like an occasional suggestion to remind you of what you've been preparing for, to keep you moving toward your goals in the discussion."

"I'm game for it," she said. "At least to try it once. Given my track record with Sam, there's nowhere to go but up."

• • • • • • •

At the beginning of the live-action session the **leader needs to sponsor your presence as her coach in the session.** This means she will define your coaching role to others who are present when she gets to the live session. Some time spent in helping her explain the role goes a long way to prevent others from thinking you are there to facilitate everyone at the meeting.

An example of a leader giving a well-sponsored explanation of the live-action role would go something like this: "I've asked Jim to be here during our conversation so he can coach me to be more effective. He has been working with me on some of my leadership goals, and improving how I conduct one-on-one conversations is one of them. Although Jim's sitting in on the discussion, he's really only focusing on how I'm doing, not you. He's raising the heat on *me* here. Jim might give me some suggestions in the middle of the conversation so I stay on track. Do you have any questions about his role?"

Live-action coaching is an art in itself. The next chapter explores more of the complexity of this particular kind of coaching.

* * * * * * *

CHAPTER SIX HIGHLIGHTS

Move the Executive to Specifics

1. Go from general venting to a particular plan.
2. Identify a next step now and check to see how it may change after looking at all five steps of the planning phase.

Help the Leader Identify Her Side of the Pattern

1. Learn how the leader habitually responds to pressure from the system.
2. Focus the leader on *her* pattern changes.
3. Help the leader connect her internal experience with her characteristic pattern.

Address Organizational and Role Alignment Issues

1. Ask the leader questions that review alignment issues.
2. Ensure the leader's strategy takes into account the alignment of roles.

Plan for Resistance to the Executive's Actions

1. Help the leader anticipate the push-back response.
2. Invite the leader to plan for internal resistance as well.

Determine Whether You Have a Live-Action Coaching Role

1. Weigh the three criteria of live-action coaching for each client.

   - The level of trust built between the coach and the executive
   - The degree to which the leader fails to see and self-correct her pattern
   - The extent to which you need calibration of the coaching because of too few signs of change in the leader

2. Clearly define the role of the coach in live action.

3. Determine with the client the range of intervention options to be used.

4. Assist the leader in preparing a sponsorship exploration of your role in the live-action session.

· · · · · · ·

· ·

Phase 3—Live-Action Coaching
Strike When the Iron Is Hot

Live-action coaching is not choreographed but is more like jazz improvisation. You intervene at unexpected yet useful times to help your client achieve his goal in the session.

Since live-action coaching means you are present when your client conducts business activities and interactions, you face a built-in awkwardness. Few people feel at ease when someone observes them doing their work. However, they begin to see the benefit when it enables them to increase their effectiveness. One new client recently told me, "I want a coach so I can see myself in action, someone who can notice what I can't."

Before exploring live action in depth, I briefly survey several types of coaching (levels 1 through 4; see Figure 7.1) in order to give you a sense of the different kinds of live-action coaching and where they are similar to and distinctive from behind-the-scenes coaching. The four levels of coaching are the following:

- Level 1: Behind the scenes—coaching the leader

- Level 2: Live action—coaching a group

- Level 3: Live action—coaching the leader in a group setting

- Level 4: Live action—coaching the leader in a one-on-one session he has with another person

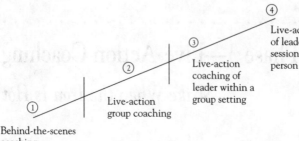

Behind-the-scenes
coaching:
contracting,
planning,
debriefing

Live-action
group coaching

Live-action
coaching of
leader within a
group setting

Live-action coaching
of leader in one-on-one
session with another
person

Figure 7.1. Range of Coaching Contexts.

These coaching contexts cover a range of experience levels from an entry (1), middle (2), and finally, highly experienced range of coaching (3 and 4). Each level requires new skills in addition to the ones of the previous levels. The last tiers of live-action coaching require higher skill sets on the part of the coach.

You can use this survey of levels to assess your skills and ascertain at what levels you are currently competent to coach executives. These levels can give you a developmental path to increase your repertoire of coaching. The more levels you can coach, the more you offer a leader.

Level 1: Behind-the-Scenes Coaching of the Leader

On one end of the coaching continuum is behind-the-scenes coaching—contracting, planning, and debriefing with the client, the focus of the previous two chapters and the subject of Chapter Eight (debriefing). Many clients may only want this kind of coaching from you. The executive implements her plan on her own without you being present. It is a bit misleading to think of behind-the-scenes coaching as the simple end of the coaching spectrum. As I have already discussed, a tremendous amount of personal presence is required. It is on the far end of the continuum, however, for two reasons: (1) It does not have the added complexity inherent in live-action coaching, and (2) it contains a required set of coaching tasks that accompany live-action coaching. Live-action coaching cannot achieve its greatest potential without contracting and planning beforehand, and debriefing afterwards.

Skills required: The skills for behind-the-scenes coaching are all those explored in the previous chapters—maintaining a strong signature presence, keeping an ability to see systems, working from the Client Responsibility Model, and helping the client set goals and plans for action.

Level 2: Live-Action Group Coaching

The next level of complexity is live-action group coaching. This is the classic group process consultation model for which organization development specialists are best known. While a leader and his team engage in a group meeting—visioning, strategizing, data collecting, planning, deciding, implementing, or evaluating—a coach/consultant intervenes in the midst of the process. By acting in the moment while events and patterns are in play, the coaching can help accelerate the team's performance and focus on their strengths. It can also help a team get back on track if they have become ineffective as a group. The live-action coach can either offer suggestions along the way, take a facilitator role in the process, or stop the meeting at critical times to conduct on-the-spot evaluation and feedback. This is classic organization development methodology.

Skills required: Besides all the skills of behind-the-scenes coaching, Level 2 requires the ability to facilitate a variety of team processes. The Client Responsibility Model has to be foremost in mind so that you do not overstep the boundaries of the coaching-facilitating role and start to manage the group in place of the leader.

Level 3: Live-Action Coaching of the Leader in the Group

The third level is live-action coaching of the leader in a group setting. As you work with the leader to help him articulate his thinking and as he puts his plan into action, you may see that his leadership and management in team meetings needs work. The leader's effectiveness in a group setting then becomes the subject of your contracting and planning sessions, as well as the focus of live-action coaching.

At first, this may seem the same as Level 2 group coaching. However, there is a subtle but substantial difference between the two. In Level 2, your client is everyone in the group—the leader or any team member. You work with everyone equally. In Level 3, your client is the executive. Unlike Level 2, you do not directly address or facilitate the group as a whole or individual members. This live-action coaching has as its focus the functioning of the leader. Your client is the leader, not the group. You do not facilitate the meeting. To the extent that you do, you deprive the leader of developmental opportunities for *him* to intervene with the group to keep it on track.

You are working specifically toward greater group leading skills in the executive. You want him to be able to accomplish his goal successfully in the meeting. It is a bit like driver's education instruction—the leader has his hands on the steering wheel of the car, not you.

Many times consultants do not use this coaching option when it could really empower their client to a new level of effectiveness. Sometimes change agents live in two extreme options of intervention—either take over the full facilitation of the group's process or coach the leader completely away from his team. Both of these methods are viable tools in themselves. Depending on them solely, however, can leave a blind spot for both leader and coach. Live-action coaching of the leader as he leads his group is just-in-time, on-the-job training of the executive where it counts— while he is in direct contact with and leading his team. This kind of live-action work combined with behind-the-scenes coaching is some of the most powerful and effective work a coach can do.

Skills required: In Level 3, you as the coach are holding a bifocal view—watching and diagnosing the quality of the group process, while directing your interventions to the executive. It takes discipline to have an opinion of how the group is doing and yet not speak directly to group members. It is not that you are holding out on their development, but you are building capacity in the leader to develop the group.

Another skill is the ability to notice the precise moment when the leader strays into his old pattern. You can then take advantage of that moment and do something to help the executive shift his pattern in real time.

One example of this live-action coaching is the work I did with Larry, the vice president of marketing, while he led his team meetings.

· · · · · · ·

Larry

Larry wanted to improve two factors in how he ran meetings: (1) get more input from team members that increased the quality of the discussions, and (2) be clearer in the meetings about defining and making decisions. We contracted for my presence at his meetings to help him with these two items.

At the beginning of the meetings, Larry let everyone know not only the agenda of the meeting, but what it was that he wanted to work on and why I was there to help him.

I had coached Larry to add one more thing: If anyone on the team noticed that he was straying from his two goals, they should speak up and mention it, not wait for me to intervene. This puts the team on notice that they are responsible for the meeting to run well and need to initiate actions to keep the meeting on track. After all, they are always there; I am not. The more they can see what they need, the more self-sufficient they become and the less they need an outside coach.

However, under Larry's leadership this group continually lost track of the discussion and was not clear about the decisions being made. A few minutes into the first agenda item, the discussion became disjointed, tangential, and unproductive. Larry did not notice or say anything to get it back on track. Instead, he became just one more group member adding to a discussion going nowhere. At that point I intervened with him by talking directly to him in front of the group so they could all hear it.

"Larry, the discussion has become disjointed—what do you want to focus on right now?"

I used a variety of live-action interventions throughout the meeting when the conversation got off track. They were all addressed to Larry. The following are some more examples:

- "A decision was just made, and I don't think there is clarity among the team what it was. Did you intend to make a decision now? Check out what people think they are committing to."

- "Are you ready to move on, or do you want to hear from more people? It's not clear what you want out of the discussion right now."

- "You have exceeded your announced time limit for this topic. Time limits aren't set in stone, but you did set it for a purpose. Make a conscious choice about this discussion rather than let it get away from you—do you want to take more time on this or close it off?"

• • • • • • •

Commenting to Larry so that everyone can hear helps break the trance of the leader's old pattern. A secondary benefit is that it can break the team's trance as well. Individual members can then contribute to the pattern change. I did not take over facilitating the meeting or change direction of the discussion. What is critical is that the decision about what to do next in the meeting remained with Larry. I kept the facilitator reins and decision-making authority in Larry's hands.

. . . .

Larry, continued

Each time I intervened, Larry took the input and then decided what he wanted to do next. At the end of the meeting Larry asked for feedback from his team about his effectiveness in leading the meeting and about when he did or did not succeed in meeting his two goals. Over time, he became more adept at running the meetings. Team members also did some of the interventions that I had typically made. I became less needed in the meeting as Larry and his team became more self-sufficient.

. . . .

In this option, the leader has contracted with you to help him get the group back on track when he loses focus. Whatever you may notice about the group's functioning is information about how you might intervene with the leader rather than with the group itself.

Level 4: Live-Action Coaching of the Leader in a One-on-One Setting

The most complicated form of live-action coaching—because of its increased intensity—is coaching the executive in a one-on-one session with someone else. There are just the three of you in the room. This level requires the leader to have a very high degree of trust in the coach and a great deal of ego strength. She has to be willing to put herself under a strong microscope in this smaller setting.

Though it would seem to be a less vulnerable forum than in front of a whole group, my experience is that executives find themselves most exposed with a coach as witness and intervener in one-on-one sessions. As a probable consequence, it is the least frequently used option.

A requirement for this kind of coaching is your track record with the executive. This type of session enables a leader to get coaching in real time while she attempts to manage her reactivity in a potentially hot situation. It is usually when the leader is most stuck with one other person that she will consider a one-on-one live coaching session. You must be able to balance respect for her authority (if she is in a manager-employee conversation) along with challenging her in real time to communicate more effectively with her staff.

Skills required: You as the coach need to do some hefty self-management in these one-on-one sessions. This is the Client Responsibility Model at its most basic and challenging level. A "hot" triangle can form when only three people are in the room and two of them have some entrenched pattern. The temptation to draw you in as interference or distraction will be great—not that they may say anything to that effect. It can be as simple as the uneasiness between the two activating your temptation to step in and rescue.

You need to maintain the bifocal view of Level 3, keeping your focus on the leader. You will feel the pull to be third-party intervener or a human resources policy expert around performance management. These roles have their place at other times, but they involve a different contract. It takes skill to discern the difference and to advise your client as to which role would best suit her development needs at the time.

Live-Action Coaching Tasks

Many of the tasks for live coaching in one-on-one sessions are used in all levels of live-action coaching, so you can apply them to Level 2 and Level 3 as well. As I go through the tasks, I use an example from Level 4 one-on-one live-action coaching. You can see that the live-action tasks follow the sequence of the tasks of the planning phase:

- **Ensure structuring of the session**

- **Follow the client's goal**

- **Foster pattern breaking**

- **Maintain alignment in the system**

Ensure Structuring of the Session

One-on-one live-action coaching can get tricky, not only for the leader but also for the other person in the session. It can seem like a dynamic of two against one (leader and coach vs. other person). Very little can be said that guarantees that this third person will feel comfortable and not intimidated by the coach's presence. **A number of tasks that structure the session can be done** on the front end, however. They show the other person that the coach is not there to be an enforcer for the client, or an arbitrator, or even a third-party facilitator.

The first task involves the **executive sponsoring the coaching,** explaining to the other person what the purpose of the session is and the purpose of the coach's presence. Your presence truly is for the leader's skill building. You do not focus on the other person or what he could be doing to improve his effectiveness.

Do not allow yourself to be a victim of your client's definition of your role. Though it is important and most effective if she sponsors your presence by defining the reason you are there, feel free to differ with and add to her definition. I tell the leader beforehand that I will augment her introduction of me if I need to. It is a way I can add my voice early in the conversation as another joining activity, rather than silently sitting there until a more intense time, when a higher impact intervention would be the first time the other person hears from me.

Someone in the other person's position is often skeptical about this at first. What is critical is that you truly live up to your purpose in the session and not focus on him midway through, no matter how tempting it is. It is also important that you show in some way that you are not in your client's "back pocket," so fused to her view of the situation that you do not have your own perspective. I often let my client know the importance of attending to this emotional landscape. I tell her that at some point in the session I will probably challenge her—when I sincerely feel the impulse—as a way of testifying to my own viewpoint.

A way to lessen the two-against-one perspective without shining a spotlight on the other person is simply to sit next to him, rather than next to the leader during the session. This gives you literally the point of view the third person has as he experiences the leader.

These small actions can add to positioning yourself as emotionally neutral to the content outcome of the conversations; you show you are not more on the side of the leader or employee in the session, even as you focus on the leader.

Follow the Client's Goals

It seems straightforward enough to be led by the goals the client established in the contracting and planning phases. Nevertheless, all kinds of distractions can divert you along the way. One big snag is the need to be useful and have something to do. You can easily think, *"Here I am, invited by the leader to sit in on this session and contribute to her effectiveness—I better not just sit here, I better contribute by **doing** something!"*

The challenge you face in live-action sessions is to be prepared to be very active at any time, while also being prepared to do nothing if that is what is called for. This is the ultimate challenge of the Client Responsibility Model of coaching. After all, it is the leader's session. "Doing nothing" *and* staying attentive and engaged takes a lot of energy. You are observing to what extent your client is accomplishing what she set out to do.

Turning your observations and your judgments into action can be difficult. I said earlier that I have a bias for action in these live-action settings. The motto from the Client Responsibility Model is "Stay Active *and* Stay Out of the Way." You want to act in the moment to increase the leader's possible learning. You can err in a number of ways, however, that actually block the leader's full learning potential. One way is to pseudo-manage, that is, fill in during all the pauses, missteps, and hesitations of the leader in such a way that you take away her leadership. You need to stay out of the way of her management of the session.

You are also not a third-party intervener. When your contract is with one party of the conversation, it is not your job to ensure that the communication or relationship of both parties is mutual or successful or resolved. Your job is to ensure that your *client* is attending to that, not that *you* make it happen—a subtle but powerful difference. The more you facilitate as a third party *when that is not what you contracted to do,* the more you increase your client's dependence on you to make it happen the next time.

So what do I do, and what does it look like?

Foster Pattern Breaking

Let's go back to the situation of the overselling director, Miriam, and the reluctant manager, Sam. We spent some planning time looking at her side of the unsuccessful pattern of their interaction. By attending to the gaps in sponsorship that were undermining her effort, she was able to get sponsorship from Jim to pull Sam out of fire-fighting situations with Ross. Miriam was now ready to address her own part in the ineffective transactional pattern with Sam. Miriam set out to **stop her own pattern as a major step,** and she wanted me to be in the session with her to help her do it differently.

• • • • • • •

Miriam in Live Action

Once we were in the live-action session, after the initial joining and structuring of the session, Miriam outlined the goal for the meeting: Settle on a course of action to turn Sam's department from one based on crisis management to one that performed well through proactive systems.

Then, leaving no room for Sam to respond to her agenda, Miriam went on automatic. She started to sell the idea of how great the new era of the department would be, how Sam would benefit, and how employee morale would increase. The more animated she was, the quieter and more sullen Sam became. In fact, he started to sit back in his chair with his feet straight out in front of him. The more she talked and gestured, the more slouched and horizontal he became in his chair.

I interrupted at that moment (somewhere between a midstream suggestion and a directive, stop-action intervention). I had enough history and trust with Miriam that I was able to say simply, "Miriam! Try something besides selling." It is as though she woke from a trance (which in some way is what a stuck pattern becomes). She stopped, and a moment of recognition flashed across her face. Then she laughed. She muttered something to herself about losing it. Then she folded her hands and said, "So Sam—this is where I am going, with Jim's support, in this division. I expect you to be a proactive manager rather than a crisis manager. Give me your ideas on how to head your department in this new direction."

Sam was silent at first, then answered in a one sentence reply. "I could talk to my supervisors and get their ideas." He stopped, still comfortably slouched in his chair. In the past, a one sentence, half-hearted reply would be enough to send Miriam back into a paragraph of selling again, and Sam could relax through another one of Miriam's monologues. This time Miriam asked, "And what good will that do?" Sam was silent again. Miriam was silent. Could she outlast Sam's silence?

After some time passed, Sam sat up in his chair and haltingly began listing some activities he and his supervisors could do. Miriam asked, "What are you willing to commit to now?" Sam paused, and then gave two priorities for action. "Fine," said Miriam. "It's a start. This is the kind of thinking I like hearing from you."

Although this result was less than stellar, it definitely was a break in the dance, one upon which Miriam and Sam could build a new pattern of interaction.

. . . .

What I *did not* do during the awkward silences was turn to Sam and interact with him; for example, "Sam, are you buying this?" or "What do you think?" or "Could you paraphrase what Miriam is telling you?" These are more along the lines of third-party work, not my contract. My goal was to help Miriam break the pattern. So I intervened through my client. It is the difference between asking Miriam if she thought Sam got what she said and asking Sam to paraphrase Miriam. The more she can stop what is not working, the more she can manage herself in this relationship without my facilitation. I was also avoiding the Rescue Model by building capacity for her independence from my interventions.

. . . .

Miriam, continued

Miriam spent the rest of the session both trying on a new pattern (making short statements followed with questions to elicit Sam's proactivity), and falling back into the old selling pattern. It was useful to her to become aware of the different ways she experienced herself in these two patterns. She saw how Sam interacted differently with her. She felt clumsy and often had difficulty finding words to fit the new pattern, but she could see the difference it created in the conversation.

. . . .

Maintain Alignment in the System

Because it is so fundamental, pattern breaking can be a powerful intervention that a leader can do to shift a situation. For increased efficacy, however, the coach needs to keep an eye on the process of organizational alignment during live-action coaching. Miriam is, after all, the sponsor and needs all of the departments within her division to be run proactively, not in a crisis mode. Such a change would recover productivity and employee morale. She needs to communicate to Sam her expectations of him as a department manager, as well as timeframes and parameters.

Therefore, what you as coach need to look for is an opportunity to **help your client change a pattern that can also support the mandate she has to exercise her authority. You are helping her align the organization to accomplish its business goals.**

This is why so much time up front is spent on establishing the bottom-line, work-process, and human relations goals. When the leader stays focused on those goals, it becomes clearer which interactional patterns need to be changed. Otherwise, there is no compass to discern whether a particular pattern is on or off the mark.

Supporting alignment in the system also recognizes the hierarchy as it shows up in the room. By that I mean refusing to take decision making away from the leader (a bad habit among change agents when they can get away with it). No matter how stumbling the leader may appear in the session, it is critical that you do not take over her job as the manager by speaking for her, establishing priorities for the employee that make sense to you, or deciding on next steps between the two of them. Maintaining alignment means staying out of the leader-employee relationship while coaching the leader to attend to that relationship, and helping her see how she can "try on" a new way of interacting with her staff.

In some ways, Miriam's selling pattern is a substitute for good old-fashioned performance management. She undercuts her own alignment to her goals through selling, which telegraphs to Sam, "You can either buy or not buy what I want you to accomplish. It's up to you." I helped Miriam live the dilemma of how to take a firm stand (backbone) while maintaining a good strong connection (heart) with those who work for her. Coaching her along this intersection is what the live-action session is all about. Interventions may take the form of directives, questions, suggestions, and debriefing on the spot—all to support the leader in creating new patterns to achieve her goals.

CHAPTER SEVEN HIGHLIGHTS

Asess Your Skill Along the Range of Coaching Contexts

- Level 1: Behind the scenes—coaching the leader
- Level 2: Live action—coaching a group
- Level 3: Live action—coaching the leader in a group setting
- Level 4: Live action—coaching the leader in a one-on-one session he has with another person

In Live-Action Coaching

1. Ensure structure of the session.
   - The executive defines and sponsors your role.
   - Position yourself for neutrality.
2. Follow the client's goals.
   - Keep the client's goals foremost when guiding your interventions.
   - Stay active *and* stay out of the way.
3. Foster pattern breaking.
   - Look for opportunities to change patterns.
   - Stay within the contract you established about how actively you will intervene.
4. Maintain alignment in the system.
   - Honor your client's authority in her system.
   - Ensure roles (sponsor, implementer, agent, and advocate) remain aligned.

Phase 4—Debriefing
Define a Learning Focus

Executives' work lives are usually structured so that they race from activity to activity. They often long for time for reflection but rarely take it due to the demands of the job. Consequently, executive coaches may need to be firm in insisting on an evaluation time in the sequence of coaching activities, and be confident themselves of the importance of this phase.

The best way to get debriefing times is to build them right into the coaching contract. Agree on times that the two of you will sit down and debrief the leader's experience. The executive needs to debrief whether you have coached behind the scenes or in live action. For example, when executives work with me in live-action coaching, their time commitment for a team meeting is not over when the team leaves the room. We spend from twenty to forty minutes evaluating their effectiveness and making plans for next steps. The method outlined here shows how to use that debriefing time effectively.

This chapter covers the following areas of debriefing:

1. Evaluate the leader's effectiveness, including

   - Assess the leader's strengths and challenges
   - Encourage executives to customize their managing
   - Review the leader's skill in management competencies

- Customize your debriefing to each executive
- Debrief with tough clients

2. Evaluate the coach's effectiveness, including
   - Build a mutual feedback loop into the coaching relationship

The first area, evaluating the leader's effectiveness, gives the leader a kind of biofeedback mechanism. He can compare his own experience to the feedback he gets from you as his coach. During the debrief phase, the executive can be open to learning and improving how he manages. Among the many items to attend to in the learning moments, I will focus on two here: the executive's approach to his employees, and his ability to enact a core set of management competencies (these can be guidelines for his future development). I will also explore ways to customize your coaching to each executive during the debriefing phase.

Sometimes, you may encounter a client who resists developing his leadership ability. In the debriefing stage, you need to decide how to continue to work with the leader—or even whether to continue to work with him at all. A section in the chapter addresses this challenge.

The last area, evaluating the coach's effectiveness, builds a sense of mutuality into the coaching contract. It is an opportunity both to get feedback from your client and to share your own assessment of your coaching in a way that models self-development.

Evaluate the Leader's Effectiveness

The process of debriefing is fairly straightforward. You start by asking your client to assess his own effectiveness. If you give your feedback first, he is more likely either to swallow it whole or defend against it, without thinking through his own response.

Assessing the Leader's Strengths and Challenges

Usually leaders focus on what they did wrong and need to improve. Insist that they speak to both areas, including what they did well, **identifying their strengths and the challenges they experienced** in their own performance in the specific situation. Keep your client's business goal front and center. Ask him if he achieved his business goal and to what extent. Reflect on what was missing. One resource of useful questions for generating greater awareness in clients is Whitmore (1996). Whitmore helps clients see their actual behaviors in a more objective light, thus encouraging them to self-correct.

After the leader gives his self-assessment, you can follow with your own feedback. To what extent do you believe he attained his goal? What are the challenges he continues to face? How effective was his leadership, and what blind spots might he be missing? The debriefing session most often falls into four categories:

- Celebration of achievements

- Identification of key recurring patterns that were either successfully broken or remained ingrained

- Assessment of the alignment of roles

- Development of a plan for the leader's next step

Celebration of Achievements

Emphasize what it is the leader did well. Executives spend very little time concentrating on their strengths—they are always looking at the gaps. While that can be a strength in itself, they need to keep in mind what they can continue doing that helps them succeed. For example, when I debriefed with Miriam, she saw two ways in which she clearly defined her expectations of Sam. She also worked to get Sam to commit to two specific action steps.

Identification of Patterns

Pattern recognition enhances the leader's ability to take a more objective look at herself, to see a larger picture and how she fits into it. Again, this activity is business focused. Rather than identifying all patterns that were played out in the situation, the leader identifies the one that most affected her results. The more she invests energy in defending against seeing her reactive patterns, the longer she will remain in a hole. A little "there I go again" view of her own defensiveness, indecisiveness, or frantic pace can help her move beyond the hole.

It helps to have a healthy dose of humor about these foibles. A coach can assist a leader in seeing that all is not lost because she tripped and fell into the same hole she knows is there in a situation. How can she put a neon sign around it for the next time? How can she notice her own internal clues more quickly? This develops an ability to have a more neutral stance toward internally stuck positions.

In debriefing, Miriam was able to feel and see the difference in herself and Sam's actions when she changed her habitual pattern with him. It allowed her to stop midstream and self-correct. This is a powerful skill for a leader to acquire.

Assessment of the Alignment of Roles

Did the executive follow the mandate in her role as a sponsor, implementer, advocate, or agent? Did she work to ensure that the other party—the team or boss or subordinate—successfully worked his own role effectively in the conversation? What loose ends, if any, around lines of authority, decision making, the goal itself, and participation still need to be clarified? Miriam realized that by getting her sponsor aligned to take Sam off fire-fighting she was able to have a much more successful session with him.

Development of a Plan for the Next Step

This kind of planning identifies a learning focus. When the leader sees how she characteristically leads, she can get bogged down by her increasing awareness of these challenges and feel immobilized.

Planning for the next action step prioritizes and breaks down these global challenges into manageable pieces, focused on the goal. It propels her into action. For example, after her session with Sam, Miriam and I talked about her next step, setting a date to follow up with Sam around his own action plan.

Encourage Executives to Customize Their Managing

After a few debriefing sessions with a leader, I sometimes see that he maintains the same approach toward all employees, no matter how different the needs or issues are. He wonders, with a lot of exasperation, why they are not coming through for him. Often, an obstacle to a leader's effectiveness is the habitual way he manages all employees, no matter who it is or what the issue may be. A coach can help leaders broaden their approaches to employees and the problems the employees face. In this situation I use Blanchard and coworkers' (1985) model of Situational Leadership because it helps leaders see the need to shift their behavior based on specific employee situations. It is a great debriefing tool because leaders experience a breakthrough that helps them choose new directions in managing others in a manner more appropriate to individuals and their specific organizational mandates.

Rather than applying a one-size-fits-all management style, Blanchard *et al.* say leaders need to match the style that brings out the best results. Managers need to assess each specific employee and the task they face at the time. Blanchard *et al.* outline different styles arising from two independent variables in the employee.

1. The **skill or competence** to do a work task.
2. The **willingness, confidence, or commitment** to do that same task.

These variables are independent because an employee can have any combination of the two; for example, he could be high in competence but low in motivation, or low in competence and high in motivation, or low in both, or high in both. A leader needs to match his leadership style to the employee's combination of the two variables.

The leader's response is based on two independent variables as well:

- Directive behaviors—predominantly one-way communication; for example, tell, explain, give directions, train, and lay out specific expectations.

- Supportive behaviors—predominantly two-way communication; for example, elicit the employee's opinions and problem-solving skills, ask for information, express empathy and respect (as defined in Chapter Five), and show confidence in the employee.

Directive behaviors are needed when an employee's competence is low; they are needed not nearly as much when it is high. Supportive behaviors are important for a low motivation or confidence level, and less crucial when an employee has high confidence or commitment.

This approach is work-task specific. For example, a leader could have an employee who has this combined profile:

- Low computer competence with low commitment to do computer tasks

- High training skills and high confidence to do the training

- Low supervisory skills with fluctuating commitment to supervise well

This employee needs different leader styles from her manager based on which task they are addressing. The leader must give high direction and high support regarding the computer tasks, low direction and low support on training skills, and high direction and high support on supervisory skills.

How can a leader keep track of all of this? Actually, it takes very little time to look at where employees stand developmentally on specific tasks. The challenge comes from the leader himself; he usually has his own preferred, dominant style, one that he keeps using on everyone, whether they need it or not.

That is where you as the leader's coach come in. **You can help executives think through their approaches with employees and evaluate whether they are effectively matching their style to what is needed.** You can spend part of the debriefing stage of coaching helping the leader learn to assess his situational leadership effectiveness.

When the leader matches his style to his employee's needs, he can accelerate the employee's development. He can also decrease the frustration they both may feel if he mismatches his style. A typical frustrating mismatch occurs when the employee is committed but unskilled and receives negligible direction and training from her boss. Another example results from an executive who constantly looks over the shoulder of a highly committed and skilled employee. Both of these scenarios can demoralize the employee and ultimately the executive.

During the debriefing phase, you can catch these typical mismatches. For example, you may notice that the leader is ignoring an employee's need for sales training but is checking up on her planning of staff coverage. Actually, she cannot do her work without the training but is quite capable of staffing her organization. You can assist the leader to take a closer look at what employees really need in each situation.

Review the Leader's Skill in Management Competencies

During debriefing sessions, you may discover the executive's level of strengths and weaknesses in a number of typical management arenas. You may find he concentrates on only a few and neglects the rest. For example, he may be good in the areas that require global thinking, but not in facilitating discussions that surface important information.

The following list of management competencies can help you scan for the areas needed to increase the executive's effectiveness in producing organizational results. Look over the skills and assess your client's ability and confidence to perform these leader activities. The list could be part of a conversation with the executive to set a developmental agenda as you continue to coach your client.

Management Competencies

Strategic thinking	Understands the whole picture. Sees complex functions from the perspective of the whole.
	Can weigh external and internal factors that affect the organization's productivity and results.
	Comprehends business issues, how an organization works.
Customer relations	Perceives the customer–vendor– internal customer (employee) –larger community (civic contexts) relationships as mutually reinforcing.
	Works to streamline processes to aid these relationships.
Vision	Develops a clear vision for self and the organization. Identifies specific and measurable goals (which are challenging, bracing, and a stretch) to achieve the vision, and communicates the vision and goals effectively.

Engages constituents in conversations to further the vision, gain greater clarity, and increase communal commitment.

Project management

Gives direction effectively. Specifically, identifies key roles, responsibilities, and timeframes of projects. Allocates the people to provide expertise and support for the projects and identifies decision makers. Clarifies the single point agent for each project. Sponsors the kickoff.

Ensures monitoring processes are in place and works to sustain cross-functional sponsorship.

Facilitating meetings

Leads meetings effectively.

Develops an agenda, prioritizing items for best use of time.

Facilitates discussion to gain maximum participation.

Helps group members identify key needs, ideas, and plans for action.

Uses a variety of group process methods to achieve effective engagement, leading to synergistic results and productive outcomes.

Decision making

Takes responsibility for clarity around who makes decisions.

	Uses several decision styles effectively; for example, consultative, delegation, consensus.
	Can firmly say yes and no and remain connected with constituents.
Utilizing staff in change agent role	Directs the work of staff agents to high-priority business issues.
	Ensures sustaining sponsors are using their agents well.
	Insists that agents remain in agent role without overstepping bounds.
Promoting conversations	Clarifies the parameters of discussions to maximize their effectiveness.
	Helps all constituencies to be heard and to speak to each other directly.
	Seeks to surface information and break habitual thinking.
	Addresses underlying issues. Talks about the tough issues.
	Takes a learning stance in conversations, that is, can expand one's position based on others' input.
Coaching	Promotes leadership and initiative in people across all roles in the organization.
	Gives specific feedback of others' strengths and weaknesses, thus

building competence and commitment in others.

Is able to train others in discreet tasks and skills relevant to their performance and increasing value, or delegate training resources to their development.

Performance management	Sets clear expectations and standards of performance for others.
	Actively holds people accountable to those standards: asks for updates; problem solves issues with participants; and enacts consequences (celebration or discipline) relevant to people's performance in an open and direct way.
Advocacy	Effectively advocates for ideas and one's part of the organization.
	Acts as an advocate to enhance the broader strategic vision of the whole organization.
	Communicates understanding and commitment to the larger goals when advocating.
Team coherence	Looks for signs of group cohesiveness or breakdown.
	Takes action to build group identity, values, and synergistic work relationships.

	Promotes the team's presence and contributions to the larger organization.
	Ensures the team has the necessary resources to perform their mandates.
	Helps the team keep a "whole system" view of their work.
Systems functioning	Expands awareness of presenting issues to include (1) the function of the organization's infrastructure, (2) the systems patterns at play, (3) the emotional tugs and pulls underlying organizational issues, and (4) the larger communities that undergird the organization.
	Includes self in the reciprocity of interactions.
	Works to increase own and others' resilience in functioning within the system and among systems.

Customize Your Debriefing of Each Executive

As you and the executive assess his skill and confidence levels in the management competencies, you will profit from using a Situational Leadership approach in your coaching. Blanchard *et al.*'s variables (competence and/or confidence; direction and/or support) also apply to leaders' capacities and motivations around management competencies.

Your clients fall into the same fluctuating set of variables as their employees. Executives' challenges have to do with accomplishing leading and managing tasks. Depending on the level of competence and commitment that executives have for the above leadership activities, you can become more or less directive and supportive in your input regarding their next steps. One example is the executive Larry, from the last chapter, who needed high direction and low support from me regarding facilitating his team meetings. He had no idea what he could do to improve, and wanted all the directives I could give him in the coaching session and during the debriefing times. Yet he needed very little support from me in terms of talking about his motivation because he was so committed to improving his leadership during meetings.

Larry had this profile in three management areas:

- Facilitating team meetings: low competence with high commitment

- Creating budgets: high competence and high commitment

- Attending to performance management: low competence and fluctuating commitment

As Larry's coach, I approached work with him very differently on each of these management tasks:

- I gave him high direction with little support needed in conversations with him about leading team meetings.

- I spent very little time on creating budgets, other than ensuring that he was clear on the parameters he had to work within his budget.

- I offered both high direction and high support on the topic of managing performance.

Do not expect to use the style of giving direction and support that falls within your own comfort zone with every executive you work with, or even consistently with any one executive. Leaders are as individual and quirky in their development as their employees. You have to match your direction and support to what they need at the time.

Debriefing with Tough Clients

The majority of clients progress on a path of greater skill in their interactions and effectiveness in reaching their business goals during coaching. There are occasions, however, when a client does not put his plans into action. When this happens, it is usually discovered in the debriefing phase if you have not coached him in live action. When the coach and client reconvene, the coach realizes that the executive is not following through.

It is important to probe enough into a leader's nonaction to discover whether the real issue is lack of confidence in his ability to make a change or some other level of threat that he thinks may result from the change. Many times seemingly "tough" clients are really leaders who are fearful, skeptical, awkward, anxious, or possess any number of attitudes that accompany a learning process. Only if these issues have been ruled out should you assume you have a "tough," nonlearning client.

Another definition of *tough* might be leaders who are cantankerous, argumentative, or dominating. But these traits can be dealt with as long as the leader is actively on a learning curve and knows that he is the key to necessary changes.

The truly tough clients say they want change but do not make it happen. They never get around to it. A case in point is Rich, the CEO in Chapter Six, who never took action but just liked to talk about his situation.

The really difficult cases are the leaders who say they are committed to changes they need to make in their management, but their automatic responses are so knee-jerk that when they get into their stressful situations they never break out to a new, more effective pattern. They stay in their reactive mode all the time and are defensive about their reactions. Then the coaching sessions cease to be productive.

OK, *you've named my coaching nightmare. But what do I do if I discover my client isn't committed? What if I have a leader who persistently does not follow through on his plan and who is not in a learning mode?* The first thing you do is to realize that you are living your worst scenario. Sometimes when you get reactive to this kind of leader, you can get into a loop of either placating or blaming him. To realize you are beginning to be in an unproductive pattern with your client is the first step out of a dance that is not working. This was the realization I made when I worked with Chris.

• • • • • • •

Chris

Chris was a can-do kind of person—smart, decisive, opinionated, and impulsive. As executive vice president in a service industry company, he juggled a lot of stores, executives, and headaches. He needed a turnaround in one of his stores and was quite critical of Jason, the general manager who ran it. When we talked about what *Chris* was doing that slowed the store's performance, he gave me a blank stare. Then the light slowly went on and he said, "I suppose I've been too tolerant." That led to a conversation of what he needed to do differently (be clearer about his expectations, and stay tuned into his relationship to Jason). We outlined a process that Chris could enact with Jason and Jason's executive team to increase productivity.

It became clear in the process that the relationship between Chris and Jason was cool and distant. Jason and his team had no consistent understanding of Chris's expectations of them. A month had gone by and Chris continued to avoid Jason. Apparently this situation was typical of Chris—when he became disappointed with someone, he distanced himself from them.

Before my next meeting with Chris, I found myself having all kinds of judgments about him. I was irritated that he hadn't followed through. How did he expect things to change? My anxiety was unusually high because it seemed that this was an entrenched pattern and things were unlikely to change. So what leverage did I have? Chris was impulsive, too. If I confronted him with this, he might write me off as well. "Oh great," I thought. "And I've got a meeting with him tomorrow morning."

Then the light bulb went on. "Wait a minute—I'm hooked," I thought. I was on the brink of distancing from Chris just as he distanced from others. And my anxiety was keeping me from more calmly sifting through the information I had in order to have a productive feedback meeting with him.

• • • • • • •

Though this realization can at first be deflating, it is actually the beginning point of taking more powerful action. That is the beauty of systemic realizations. When you know a system's pattern has caught you, that change in perspective can lead to a way out.

One way out is to ask, *"What would I do if I weren't hooked and my client was open?"* In other words, if you were at your best and this were a client on a learning curve, what would you be doing? These questions help to clear your thinking from your knee-jerk fight-or-flight reactions. A challenging situation like this needs you at your best; your client is responding automatically and is currently unable to create a new outcome.

This is not Pollyanna thinking. It is challenging yourself to what the role of executive coach requires of you, which in this moment is giving straightforward feedback to the leader.

What has often been helpful to me in these situations is thinking about the central pattern at play. I name it as a theme or headline, as neutrally as possible, to the leader. I then give my position relative to that theme. In other words, I give the executive my best thinking on what is required in this situation.

In a case like that with Chris, this approach keeps me from distancing from him, even as we are going through some rough water. I continue to partner with him by giving him creative approaches to the issue. I also need to identify my bottom line and ask myself what I am willing or not willing to do with this client, including perhaps terminating the contract if he does not show enough movement toward change. Ending the contract does not come as a punishment or an emotional cutoff. It is a regretful and respectful termination, rather than a harsh one, and comes from a realization we cannot do any further fruitful work without a significant change in the client.

In summary, the tasks of dealing with a tough, apparently non-learning client are the following:

- **Identify the central pattern.**
- **Give the leader your best thinking on the issue.**
- **Identify and communicate your personal bottom line of involvement with the client.**

Here is how these tasks played out with Chris:

. . . .

Chris, continued

In my meeting with Chris, I reported to him what I knew about what he had done and not done. I asked him whether he had anything different or more to report. No additions. Neither was he forthcoming in committing to do anything differently. He seemed to be waiting for me to come up with interesting thoughts about Jason's deficiencies and discuss what Jason would have to do to change.

"Chris," I said, "you are continuing to keep a safe distance from Jason (*name the pattern*). And you are setting him up to fail. It's like you're at a gunslingers' standoff—you're facing him from a careful distance, and neither of you is making a move. Now, what usually happens in these situations is that it continues until one of you can't stand it any longer, and then you blow each other's head off. No communication, then blasto! What I also know is that that doesn't lead to increased productivity. One or both of you will be casualties for not engaging with each other. Ultimately, his productivity is affecting your productivity (*give best thinking*). Do you really want to go down with him over this? If you are not willing to change your work relationship with Jason, I can no longer be useful to you" (*personal bottom line*).

Chris hadn't been thinking about his own vulnerability in the situation. That actually got him more motivated to address the issue with Jason. His new awareness of his self-interest raised his energy to push against his own resistance to change.

· · · · · · · ·

This tough client turned around enough to be in a learning mode and began to change his behavior. The story does not always end this way. Some clients do not take the action they need. No matter what the context, debriefing your experience of your client with him is as necessary a step in the methodology as the other phases.

Evaluate the Coach's Effectiveness

At some point in the client-coach relationship, you should include an evaluation of your effectiveness as a coach. A natural time for that to happen is during the debriefing phase. This builds **a feedback loop in the working relationship** and ensures that you are serving the client well. A side benefit is your powerful modeling of someone initiating and receiving feedback and being in a learning mode.

When you debrief your effectiveness, **it is important for the client to give his feedback to you first.** This offers you the experience of being on the receiving end of this leader's feedback, an experience you now share with others in the workplace. You can then take the opportunity to give him feedback on his feedback (talk about immediacy!). Usually he needs to be more specific and more balanced with strengths and suggestions.

When you assess your work with the executive, you can model learning from experience and demonstrate that current results are the basis from which to build greater achievement.

The degree of your candor with your client about your strengths and weaknesses depends on the strength of your working relationship. With new clients it is important to establish credibility about your effectiveness before launching into a litany of your weaknesses. Even though you may be fully confident that you are giving leaders effective service, they turn skittish if you self-assess too thoroughly. First of all, the session is supposed to be about them, not you. Second, it comes across as a lack of confidence in your skills. This obstacle quickly fades, however, when the leader sees that you can be effective *and* continually assess your coaching.

In debriefing your coaching, you can **identify your own strengths and weaknesses** of the coaching partnership. Once they trust you, clients are sometimes pleasantly surprised by the candor, which can help them to be more open as well. This includes **reviewing the ways you may have become stuck in patterns** that were not useful to the leader. You may have fallen into the same dance patterns of the system, or contributed to a pattern between the leader and yourself that took away from your effectiveness with him. Some examples of a self-assessment review may include the following:

Strengths

- "I helped you get crisper in articulating your goals."

- "I stayed on top of your dominant pattern with you and your team and was able to help you catch yourself in two critical moments."

Weaknesses

- "I backed off from pushing you around measures, which left you vulnerable in the meeting with your boss."

- "I underestimated what a challenge it was for you to manage the other person in the meeting. We could have specifically strategized for it."

Besides offering good modeling, your self-assessment also helps the leader prioritize what he wants to continue to improve. For example, after listening to your self-report, he may decide to put more effort into managing the other person in the meeting.

The last part of debriefing, therefore, is **recontracting.** Since this is a continuing relationship, it is useful after a piece of work to recycle through the steps. This can mean shifting the contract to fit the leader's new or continuing goals, not assuming that what he needs now is the same as before. It is also the time to **revisit the measures for the goals of the initial contract, to see to what extent the outcomes have been attained.** The whole phase of debriefing can help the client build a capacity to continue these action research phases on his own.

* * * * * * *

CHAPTER EIGHT HIGHLIGHTS

Evaluate the Leader's Effectiveness

1. Discuss client's strengths and challenges.

2. Identify key recurring patterns.

3. Assess the alignment of roles.

4. Plan the leader's next step.

Encourage Executives to Customize Their Managing

1. Help leader diagnose individual employees' development needs.

2. Ensure leader matches management style to the development needs of employees.

Review the Leader's Skill in Management Competencies

1. Scan for management skills that the leader needs to strengthen.

2. Build a development plan for the executive that addresses these areas.

Customize Your Debriefing of Each Executive

1. Recognize the development needs of the executive you coach.

2. Match your coaching style to the leader's level of competence and confidence.

Debriefing with Tough Clients

1. Identify the central pattern at play.

2. Give the leader your best thinking on the issue.

3. Communicate your personal bottom line.

Evaluating Coach Effectiveness

1. Ask for feedback from the client first and follow with your own self-assessment.

2. Identify your strengths and challenges as a coach.

3. Identify patterns you participated in.

4. Recontract for further coaching.

* * * * * * *

Part III

. . . .

Special Applications

• •

Making a Strategic Transition to the Role of Executive Coach

This chapter is for those of you who are organizational consultants and trainers and who want to move more into the role of executive coach from where you are right now. This assumes that you have the necessary **traits of an executive coach**—those that have been explored in the book, such as the following:

- You hold a systems perspective.

- You have a strong sense of self. You are not intimidated by people in positions of authority.

- You can work in the middle amid others' anxiety.

- You are business and results focused.

- You are an excellent listener.

- You can move conversations from the global to the specific.

- You can give immediate feedback.

- You are equally able to support and challenge.

- You have a sense of humor about human foibles.

- You can let others create their own successes and mistakes.

You may be working in companies with dozens of leaders throughout the organization, yet none are asking you for coaching, even though you have the skills to be an executive coach. This was exactly my situation when I was director of training for a corporation. Here was a team of seven executives and twenty-five other leaders who directed the efforts of the organization. However, I was not hired to coach them. Initially, I was expected to carry out training duties for the organization. Offering to coach anyone, let alone the top executive, would have seemed absurd to them. Then later I found myself in the enviable position of being sought out as a coach by those executives on strategic and tactical issues for the organization.

You can bridge the gaps between your current situation and the more developed coaching relationships you want in your practice. Typical questions and dilemmas people have in making this transition include the following:

- What do I do when I have a leader who doesn't know how to use me as a coach?

- How do I start from where I am now? How do I create an opportunity?

- What if the leader has a completely different map for change and my role within that change?

- How do I deal with the leader's resistance to spending time on coaching?

- How do I get the leader to see me differently?

- How can I ensure the leader has a first successful experience of me as her coach?

- What do I do when I have a good idea before the sponsor does?

- How do I deal with an "inadequate" or weak leader?

- How can I help the leader to see my coaching role as leverage for her to reach greater effectiveness?

These concerns about role expectations boil down to three things:

- Anxiety that you do not see eye-to-eye with your sponsor about what your **role** should be.

- The need to get the right **contract** for coaching, so you can be successful with the executive and, therefore, help her to be successful.

- The skill and presence needed to get into the **right conversation with the leader** in order to address the first two concerns.

Concerns over Your Role

There are tip-offs that indicate your sponsor does not see your role in the same way you do. When you offer to coach her on her leadership dilemmas, she gives you a quizzical, somewhat impatient look, which leaves you squirming. Or she approaches any work with you from the Rescue Model. She wants you to take things into your own hands rather than help her address them. You might encounter comments such as these:

- "So, what have you got to get this implementation off the ground?"

- "Just go tell them that the deadline is unacceptable."

- "Why are you coming to me when you need to be spending your time getting the team going?"

These reactions and others like them indicate a mismatch in understandings about your role. They come from a leader who is not considering her own responsibilities to continue strong sponsorship in a change initiative. She will often assume you should be doing activities that from a Client Responsibility perspective are really her responsibility as a sponsor and not yours as a change agent. The last thing she thinks of is the resource you are to her *as a coach* to help her think through and maintain those sponsor activities— ensuring alignment throughout the organization, communicating commitment to a goal, clarifying decision authority with key players, and providing resources.

The Contract

This situation cries out for ensuring that you get **the right contract** as a change agent in the project, including clarifying what you can do as an executive coach. You know you have the right contract when the leader and you are both working from the same page, that is, the Client Responsibility Model. The leader understands her responsibilities as sponsor and sees you as a resource to keep her honest about them. The more you both operate from this same model, the more you will find yourself coaching the leader. You may also be asked to do other duties as change agent to help get a project under way. The agentry work that comes from those requests will be better leveraged and more effective when it is in tandem with responsibilities the leader maintains herself.

Here are a couple of common questions and complaints about leaders:

- *What if my sponsor does not know the Client Responsibility Model? Do I have to teach it to her?*

- *I have an inadequate sponsor who doesn't take a look at his responsibilities but thinks of plenty of activities to dump off on me.*

Very few people are born great sponsors—they have to develop into the role. Some sponsors are lucky enough to connect with a great coach who can develop them. The coach does this by being an effective change agent who evokes stronger sponsorship from the leader. Rather than looking at the inadequacy of your sponsor, perhaps the question is, "Are you being a great change agent?"

The Conversation

No, you do not have to teach your sponsor the Client Responsibility Model. It's worse than you think—you have to embody it, using no fancy jargon. This requires getting into **the right conversation** with the executive. It means moving *with* your sponsor to the Client Responsibility perspective, not jumping there yourself and then blaming her for staying unknowingly in the Rescue Model. It starts with your ability to manage yourself in your relationship with the sponsor. First focus on acting differently with her, rather than waiting for her to act differently with you.

Guidelines for the Conversation

There are several guidelines to keep in mind that we will explore here. You may recognize them from other chapters. They help you stay on a path that increases your success of entering and staying in conversations that promote your coaching skills.

- Act *as though* you and the sponsor are both already in the Client Responsibility Model.

- Focus on the leader's goals.

- Provide a sample of what you can offer: Demonstrate it right in the conversation.

- Find a way to say yes to the leader's goals.

- Have goals for managing yourself in the conversation.

- Offer loyal resistance—a form of advocacy—if necessary.

In acting as though you are in the Client Responsibility Model, always think about how you can help the leader see her responsibility to keep a strong connection with her people and be clear with her expectations. Define what you can do with her to assist her in building greater clarity and stronger relationships. Act *as though* your sponsor is capable of joining you in this perspective, *even if she has never demonstrated this ability before.*

What do you actually talk about? **Build credibility as a business partner** by talking about business goals and results. Then **link business challenges to the leader's challenges.** This provides a natural **segue to executive coaching.** Therefore, you need to **discuss the leader's goals, not your aspirations to coach.** Engage them in what they care about. You need to define your role within the context of what they are motivated to achieve. What you want to accomplish professionally is *not* what they stay up nights thinking about. Concentrating on anything besides what preoccupies them is essentially counterproductive to your own interests. Focusing on the self-interest of the other person will get you further than trying to sell them on something more related to what you want. This is a realistic approach to leaders—they sponsor best what they care about. Expand their horizons by linking new issues, insights, and your capabilities to their passions, concerns, and interests.

Once you find yourself talking with a leader about her goals, here are some typical questions to ask her to get more deeply into the conversation (Schachter, 1997, p.1):

What do you want to accomplish in this effort?

What is your best thinking about this issue?

Have you met this challenge successfully before?

What are the gaps in meeting the same kind of challenge this time?

How urgent are you about this issue?

How do you account for not being able to accomplish this?

Do you have any sense of what your part is in not meeting the challenge this time?

In your position as the leader, what challenges do you personally feel to pull this off?

What outcomes do you want?

What would be achievable results in what specific timeframe?

To what extent do the people who report to you hold the same perspective or urgency that you have?

Does your team know as much about what you're thinking as I know now?

You probably recognize these questions as conversation starters for the contracting phase of coaching. That is exactly the phase you are in when you are in the right conversation to further develop your coaching.

By asking these questions you can go a long way in developing the leader's thinking about her relationship with her team and the expectations she has of them. *Congratulations—just by asking these goal and team relationship questions you begin to serve in an executive coaching capacity.*

However, you do not define the discussion beforehand as a coaching conversation. That would scare off many leaders. You give them the experience first. You are giving your potential coaching "customer" a sample of what you can do. The experience, plus a debriefing of the conversation afterward (what was helpful about it, what further clarity does she have, and so forth), gives you a beginning track record of executive coaching with that particular leader. Later, you can point to these experiences and offer to have more of these kinds of conversations about the projects the leader finds particularly challenging. To the extent that you have managed well your relationship with the executive, she will likely take you up on your offer.

Find a way to say yes to the leader's goals. Most consultants who are executive coaches also carry other change agent responsibilities: facilitating, training, data gathering, mediation, and project management. Sometimes what the sponsor wants you to do in these other roles flips you both back into the Rescue perspective. This is the critical moment in the sponsor-agent relationship. *Find a way to say yes to her goal, by redefining for her what your change agent tasks could be to help her achieve her goal.* Articulate your role and responsibilities in the light of the sponsor's goals and responsibilities. Talk about how both of your roles interplay with each other.

What kind of dialogue can you have that attends to both of your roles, working to align them? An example of this kind of conversation is the following (it also gives your sponsor a "heads-up" on chances for success):

AGENT: You say you want the managers to enact the new performance standards.

LEADER: You got it.

AGENT: And you want me to train them on the new approach.

LEADER: I can't think of a better person to do the job.

AGENT: And you are saying you are unable to take time before the training to talk to the managers concerning their reservations about the new system.

LEADER: You've seen my schedule! We've barely had time for this conversation.

AGENT: Don't get me wrong—I'm happy to do the training. But let me lay out what I think would be the chances of this training "sticking" with the managers. They will know how to do it, but without you dealing with their concerns, you have a less than 40 percent chance of getting an organization-wide system in place. If you deal with their concerns beforehand, even if that means having some tough discussions about it, you dramatically increase your chance of getting an organization-wide rollout of the standards.

LEADER: Increase it by how much?

AGENT: You call the shots on that one. You decide what percentage you're satisfied with. You work their commitment until you get the percentage you want.

LEADER: Why don't you just explain the need for it at the start of the training?

AGENT: Even if I said it eloquently they would continue to covertly resist you by not doing it. Hearing me talk about it is no substitute for getting it directly from you. And you know what? They deserve that from you.

LEADER: You sure know how to increase my workload.

AGENT: It's a pay-me-now or pay-me-later system. You either deal with their commitment on the front end, or try to get it from them later while the project unravels. The second option takes up more of your time, as you and I have both painfully learned from past experience.

This kind of conversation requires your signature presence in managing yourself in the white water of the leader's urgency, anxiety, and impatience. You are successful the more you can have the conversation without blaming the sponsor for her shortcomings, or giving up on her for being stubbornly resistant to the idea of strongly sponsoring the change she wants. At every chance to blame or give up on her, you can stay the course of your position, offering it as neutrally as you can, as information that you believe is useful to her. You are painting pictures and outcomes that the sponsor most cares about; for example, an organization-wide change in implementing standards. You describe your role relative to the role you see her playing that will get her the results she wants.

It is also important to ask the leader to respond to your position. What is her best thinking about what you just said? What are its merits, and what are her nagging concerns?

AGENT: So what do you think about what I just said?

LEADER: OK, OK, I see your point. I can't wiggle out of this one. But I still don't see how I'm going to pull this off—I haven't got the time for it!

AGENT (*here is a critical juncture in the conversation—do you rescue the leader from her responsibility or continue to let her struggle with it?*): You're in a tough spot. And you know what strikes me as ironic? Lack of time to implement is exactly one of the managers' reservations about this new system. You are struggling with what they are struggling with. The more you deal with your own challenges on how to make this a priority, the more you can be a resource to the managers on how they can make it a priority in their work. And the more you raise this as a common dilemma among all of you, the more you will build your connection with them around this issue.

LEADER: That's a tall order.

AGENT: That's what you and I can talk about—how you're going to fill that tall order (*the coaching opportunity*).

The critical juncture occurs in this conversation when the change agent might have gotten distracted by the leader's frustration. Instead, the agent stays the course by keeping the challenge front and center with the leader, **bringing immediacy to the conversation** (her time constraint being the same issue that the managers face).

The more you find these moments of immediacy—that the very pattern the leader wants to be different out there is happening in your conversation, here and now, with her—the more powerful your coaching will be, and the more apt the leader is to see you as a coaching resource. Using immediacy segues to the *real* issue of how daunted the leader feels in dealing with time pressures and her management team.

As this example demonstrates, you can have a jargon-free conversation while operating within the perspective of the Client Responsibility Model. One of the model's requirements is to stay on the task of building the sponsor's responsibility, even while you are anxious and under some heat yourself to rescue her from that responsibility. You do not have to be eloquent or graceful, just effective.

The kinds of conversations I have been promoting in this chapter are what I call **coaching moments.** They happen outside the context of a formal coaching contract but *within* the context of the leader's work world and high-priority concerns. Opportunities to have these conversations are plentiful. They happen as the executive is focused on something else. They build credibility in you as a resource for the leader in ways she may not have at first imagined. Coaching moments can cover some of the same territory as the coaching phases, though in smaller increments. You can still

- Listen well to the leader.

- Help her get more clarity about what the issue is, the goal she wants to accomplish, and a next step.

- Give feedback of your experience of her in the dilemma that can shed light on how she is leading this particular effort.

These moments over time build your portfolio of coaching skills that can later develop into more formal coaching relationships.

Having goals for managing yourself within this kind of conversation is essential for staying on task (these are the same as the process goals from Chapter Two). Goals keep you from getting sidetracked by your own anxiety in the face of the leader's impatience or irritation. Here are some examples of goals that I have maintained for myself, taken from several of these kinds of meetings in the past:

- When the leader gets impatient, focus on results.

- Don't jump into an awkward silence. Let the leader take initiative in this conversation.

- Stick with only one personal bottom line. Don't complicate the picture with too many requirements from my side.

- Find a moment to be immediate—the pattern "out there" is going on in here between us.

- She doesn't need to hear how this project complicates my life—tell her whether or not I think it will work.

- Don't speak for other people. Speak for myself and invite her to seek out the opinions of others.

I do not have all these goals in each meeting. They are tailored to the leader, the situation, and my particular anxieties at the moment. It is best to have only one or two of them in a specific conversation.

Loyal Resistance

You may notice a tone that comes through in the example conversation and in these sample goals for the coach. It is what I call *loyal resistance*. When a leader is choosing methods or approaches that I judge to be counterproductive to the very direction she wants to take, I initiate my loyal resistance.

Loyal resistance is a form of advocacy. Actually, many of the activities I have suggested in this chapter—**focusing on the leader's goal, tying your role and aspirations to what they want to achieve, finding a way to say yes**—are forms of effective advocacy. As you recall from Conner's definition (Chapter Four), **advocacy** means promoting an idea, solution, or role that you are excited about so the leader sponsors it as something she wants and owns as well. Loyal resistance occurs when a leader wants something from me that I cannot support because of an incongruence with my values or my skepticism that it will work.

With loyal resistance you are putting yourself out there as clearly standing in a different, sometimes opposing place from the leader. However, since your intent is not to polarize your position with the leader, you show your willingness to join the deeper interest she holds. In loyal resistance you do three things simultaneously:

1. **Get on board the leader's train.**
2. **Articulate clearly your difference with her approach.**
3. **Offer alternatives that can satisfy her interest and deal with your concerns as well.**

When you use this triple focus, you are invaluable to your sponsor.

Getting on board the executive's train shows the leader that you deeply understand *what* she is trying to accomplish. You do it through the activities already mentioned—focusing on her goal and finding a way to say yes to her interest behind the goal.

The tricky part is most often **articulating your differences** with her approach, *how* she wants to get there. You need to be thoughtful about your own perspective and have weighed its merits and obstacles carefully. The more you can offer your viewpoint as useful information, rather than a crusade or battle for the "right" position, the more likely it is that the leader will listen to you. This is particularly true when you tie your thinking to the executive's outcomes. You can save a leader from herself by highlighting what she may not be noticing in the situation. In these circumstances, if you do not share your knowledge and reservations, you are holding out on the leader, withholding your best thinking from her.

When you add the third ingredient in loyal resistance, you add power to your position. **Offer alternative solutions** that address your concerns while fulfilling what the leader wants to accomplish. After all, executives are most interested in getting to a destination, not in the path to go there. Presenting ideas in tune with their agenda can sometimes open leaders up. The ensuing brainstorm can generate options no one had yet mentioned, and the conversation gains renewed synergy. You show, again, how valuable you are as a business partner. Leaders are very attracted to people who can join them in commitment to their goals, *and* bring their differences, *and* offer alternative ways of thinking about an issue.

Once you and your sponsor are in the right conversation, you build your experience base as an executive coach. Success is established by hundreds of these small conversations. You may start out with fifteen minute discussions that veer in this direction. If you are just embarking on the adventure of coaching leaders, do not sabotage yourself by expecting to have full-blown, brilliant, lengthy executive coaching conversations the first time out. Do not call it executive coaching until your have a track record with the leader. You need time to evolve your role; and the leader needs time to make changes in herself and to develop her understanding of your role with her.

• • • • • • •

CHAPTER NINE HIGHLIGHTS

Identify the Leader's Understanding of Your Role

1. Look for misalignment in expectations about your role between you and the leader.

2. Avoid taking on Rescue Model activities.

Get the Right Contract

1. Work for sponsor-agent alignment.

2. Ensure that all your change agent duties come from the Client Responsibility Model.

Get in the Right Conversation

1. Increase your ability to evoke stronger sponsorship in the leader.

2. Use the following guidelines for the conversation:
   - Act *as though* you are in the Client Responsibility Model.
   - Talk about the leader's goals.
   - Provide a sample of what you offer.
   - Find a way to say yes to the leader's goals.
   - Find moments of immediacy.
   - Have goals for managing yourself.
   - Offer loyal resistance—a form of advocacy—if necessary: partner with the leader's goals, articulate your differences, *and* offer alternative ways of thinking about the issue.

◆　◆　◆　◆　◆　◆

10

. . . .

Helping Leaders Effectively
Coach Employees

A s a coach to executives, you often work with leaders to help them become better coaches to their employees. Much of the perspective of this book and the coaching phases are applicable for leaders who want to coach more effectively. However, leaders have special and distinct management responsibilities they need to accomplish in conjunction with coaching.

In this chapter I explore areas of concern you need to address when you help a boss become a better coach. One is **role clarity,** a clear articulation of the two roles the leader takes on in coaching employees. The other deals with an effective **sequencing of role responsibilities** toward the employee involved in a coaching situation.

Role Clarity

When leaders coach, they commonly make the mistake of downplaying their role as the employee's boss. This creates confusion in the employee and unproductive coaching on the part of the boss. An executive who wants to coach his employees must keep his roles clear. A boss is a sponsor. A coach is an agent. As I mentioned earlier in Chapter Four, it is possible to play multiple roles, to be both a sponsor and an agent. However, an executive has to be clear about the hat he wears at any given time, as a way to manage **the complexity created by the dual role.**

For example, a boss is the one who holds people accountable for results. A coach helps people increase their skills to achieve the results. A boss-coach is someone who both mandates the goal and helps people develop the ability to accomplish it. A boss cannot pretend *not* to have performance expectations of his employees while he is coaching them. His performance expectations are always there.

There are common pitfalls when people act as both a boss and a coach. One extreme is the boss who soft-pedals his bottom-line expectations because as a coach he wants to develop his employees. A boss may try to "coach" an employee into compliance (replace the word *coach* with *nag, cajole,* or *plead*). This faulty thinking goes something like this, "Maybe if I coach them, they'll do what I want." Coaching is not a substitute for performance management. Yet another extreme is a boss who thinks coaching means being directive and giving an employee mandates on how to accomplish expectations.

Therefore, there are *separate and sequential tasks* a boss needs to do with any employee:

> **Task 1: Name performance expectations and ensure employee commitment to them.**
>
> **Task 2: Coach and develop employees to accomplish those expectations.**

Leaders should not confuse the two duties, and the first task *must* be done before the second. Task 1 places the leader's coaching within a larger context that ties it to clarifying work expectations. Trying to coach without first attending to the boss's expectations is wasted coaching time and produces poor results. Your job as an executive's coach is to help a leader through this sequence so he can incorporate coaching effectively within his management responsibilities.

Task 1: Name Expectations and Ensure Employee Commitment

Many managers live by the "read-my-mind" school of management —they are not explicit enough with their expectations. Then they wonder why they are not getting the results they need when they "coach" employees. The leader's first job as a boss is to be clear about his expectations and gain employee commitment to those expectations.

Clarity in expectations means being behaviorally specific. The employee needs to know

- *What* the leader wants accomplished,

- By *whom*,

- By *when*,

- How much *decision-making authority* the employee has to accomplish the goal.

Here is an example of clear and specific expectations:

> I want you to head up the task force on new employee orientation. John, Bill, Jane, and Sue will work with you (*who*). I want you to come back with a program, the length of time each new employee is needed for it, and a draft training manual (*what*). You have two months to make a recommendation to me (*when*). I want the task force team to have majority vote on the specifications of your recommendation (*decision-making authority*).

Here is another example:

> You have to start handling the conflicts that come up in your department, instead of people coming to me to

resolve them. Beginning immediately, *(when)* you *(who)* will ensure disagreements are resolved so that your staff are only coming to me with issues that are outside your control *(decision-making authority)*. In fact, I want you to be the one who comes to me with those issues *(who)*.

When the leader has clarified his expectations with an employee, he dramatically raises the employee's chance of success, as well as the leader's. For more on giving explicit and specific expectations, see Fournies (1998).

Just because the executive has been clear, however, does not mean the employee gladly accepts the task and implements it. Sometimes an employee resists the leader's expectations, either explicitly through argument, or covertly through lack of follow-through.

Task 1 also includes gaining commitment from the employee, an essential step before moving on to Task 2. An employee's commitment is shown in three ways:

- **Understanding the goal.**

- **Emotionally committing to the goal.**

- **Taking initiative toward the goal.**

Without all three items in place, coaching an employee is premature.

Understanding

The employee needs to clearly communicate her understanding of the business goal. Even if the employee does not agree with it, it is important that she understands *what* is being required of her and the priority of importance the leader places on it. It is often useful to ask the employee to paraphrase her understanding of the leader's expectations back to him.

Commitment

Understanding is a necessary but insufficient criterion. An employee must also communicate her ownership for accomplishing a business goal. As long as she sees the goal as the leader's issue and not hers, the first task is incomplete. The leader needs the employee's commitment to the goal so the leader does not have to berate, coax, or beg her. She needs to make it as much a priority in her work as it is for the leader. Employees show commitment when they begin to speak of the goal as a regular part of their work. They let the full weight of the goal's implications sink into their awareness. Appropriately, they take on some of the anxiety of responsibility for it. They accept the management of the positive and negative consequences of the project.

Initiative

With commitment comes initiative. The leader knows the employee is ready when she spends energy addressing the issues and obstacles inherent in the business goal, and is motivated to see it successfully completed. She brings her own ideas and communicates them to the leader without him having to solicit them.

Sometimes a leader is eager or anxious to get on with a project, and will settle for one or two of the criteria instead of all three. This is where you as the leader's coach come in. You can continue to challenge the leader to be thorough in the first task so the rest of his work does not unravel later on down the road; and you can be particularly useful when the process does not go smoothly, when the leader runs into an employee's resistance.

Dealing with Resistance

When an employee balks at a leader's performance expectations, one of three things may be at play:

1. **A lack of skill or confidence to accomplish the business goal.**

2. **A legitimate concern about organizational obstacles or priorities that interfere with performance of the goal.**

3. An unproductive leader-employee pattern that distracts the employee from the goal.

The first is a legitimate coaching issue and can be addressed in the second task—coaching for increased performance. The last two must be addressed during Task 1 before moving on to coaching. Let's explore these three areas of resistance.

Lack of Skill or Confidence

The employee actually is not resisting the expectation but doubts her ability to accomplish it, or may in fact not be trained to do it. This does fall into the coaching category because the employee understands the expectations, can be emotionally committed to them, and lacks initiative only because of the skill-confidence issue, not because of a lack of agreement.

The leader can use the Situational Leadership model to tailor his coaching to the specific employee's needs around the issue of confidence-competency to do the task. In fact, you can serve your client well by developing his diagnosis ability in determining the employee's developmental needs. Then the leader can match his coaching style to fit those needs.

There are times when an employee is totally unfamiliar or unskilled in a key process that would accomplish the goal. **Training** becomes necessary in these situations. For an employee to be productive, the executive needs to offer all the classic stages of training:

- Demonstrate the task.

- Explain how to do it.

- Observe the employee doing it.

- Give feedback on her performance, repeating the steps if necessary.

Employees are short-changed when they do not receive all of the training steps. Manager-coaches are responsible for making sure that they or someone they designate give the employee the skills necessary to her job mandate.

A Legitimate Concern About Organizational Obstacles

An employee may in her resistance bring up issues about the structure of the organization, contradictory priorities, or resource problems that need to be addressed up front. If they are not addressed, the employee's efforts may fail no matter how committed she is.

Many times the leader does not want to hear about these obstacles, but he must if the goal is to be successfully accomplished. This is actually an example of the loyal resistance I mentioned in Chapter Nine. The employee's objections are an effort to improve the organization and can lead to an appropriate readjustment of the leader's expectations. This loyal resistance is good feedback to the manager. He needs to be clear with the employee what he will do to better structure the project so that the employee can accomplish her mandate. For more on the conversation between a manager and employer on organizational obstacles, see the "Improving Performance" section of Kinlaw (1993).

An Unproductive Leader-Employee Pattern

A third reason an employee resists a leader's direction has more to do with an unproductive, long-established pattern between the two of them. There may be an unintentional but quite ingrained habit of relating with each other that increases the employee's resistance to the leader's direction. It happens more often than most executives think. If the executive tries to coach the employee before they break the pattern, he actually reinforces the problem and continues to thwart progress toward the business goal. You can **coach the leader to look for and identify his unproductive**

pattern with this employee. Some possible patterns include the following:

- The leader raises concerns, and the employee attempts to talk him out of those concerns.

- The leader invites, and the employee declines.

- The leader brings up issues that feed the fears of the employee who then gets paralyzed rather than mobilized.

- The leader threatens, and the employee threatens back.

- The leader enthusiastically sells a great idea, and the employee becomes a passive buyer (à la Miriam and Sam's pattern).

Missing from all these patterns are straightforward performance expectations. Expectations do not exist in a vacuum but within a relationship. The leader–employee relationship pattern can make it difficult to give straightforward expectations. As the leader's coach, strongly advise against coaching (Task 2) until this pattern is shifted.

There is, of course, the issue of homeostasis, the push-back to any pattern change. As the leader changes his side of the pattern—stops inviting, or stops raising concerns, or stops threatening, or stops feeding fears—and starts being more clear and straightforward, the leader will get resistance to the very change he makes. He might say, "First she won't do it, and now she's fighting my shift in the approach I'm taking with her!" This double dose of resistance is common before the leader and employee establish a more productive pattern. The leader has to learn to expect this kind of resistance and increase his own tolerance level for it so that he does not return to the old pattern because the employee's resistance makes him uncomfortable.

You can help the leader plan for this kind of resistance and explore options to increase his tolerance in the face of it. Here are **guidelines you can give the leader.** He can take this sequence of actions to help gain an employee's commitment and initiative when facing an unproductive pattern between them:

- The leader **clearly states his business goal and measurable outcomes.** He is specific and thorough in his expectations.

- The leader **stays the course** in his position through the storm of the employee's resistance in attempting to maintain the old pattern. The leader anticipates the employee's push-back and stays on track anyway. This is the backbone part of managing.

- The leader **reinforces the change** in the employee's side of the pattern when she has joined the leader with a more productive response. How is she showing her change? Through her (1) understanding of the goal, (2) committing to the goal, and (3) taking initiative toward the goal. Now that is something the leader can work with!

This gets the leader to the starting gate of coaching (for an example, reread the conversation between Miriam and Sam in Chapter Seven). You can insist that the leader proceed only when the employee understands and commits to the business goal.

Task 2: Coaching for Increased Performance

Once the employee is ready for coaching, the leader can use the coaching phases mentioned in Chapters Five through Eight, including contracting, planning, live-action coaching, and debriefing.

Contracting

Contracting from a boss position covers some of the same ground as agent coaching: **The leader familiarizes himself with the employee's challenge** and examines what it looks like from the employee's point of view. The leader helps the employee **get specific about the issue.** What in particular is difficult for her? What are the obstacles? What has she tried already? It is important to keep the ownership with the employee, just as it was for the executive coach to keep ownership with the client.

The executive also **tests the employee's willingness to reflect on the part she may be playing.** Can she see how she contributes to her dilemmas around the business issue? The leader **uses immediacy** and describes his experience of the employee while he talks with her. This feedback holds up a mirror on the employee's attitudes and actions. Finally, the executive establishes a contract to coach. Once Task 1 (which is mandatory) is completed, Task 2—coaching—is an option that the employee can accept or decline. This optional approach positions the employee's motivation where it belongs— with her. She takes advantage of whatever tools she believes she needs to help her, including the coaching she gets from her boss.

Planning

During the planning phase of coaching, the executive helps the employee determine her next step. There may be a pattern the employee is stuck in when dealing with the business issue; she may habitually approach or avoid the issue in ways that keep her from forging ahead. The leader helps the employee **identify her pattern.** Then the leader helps her **identify her specific next step,** particularly changing her side of the pattern. Some examples of employees naming their patterns are

- "Every time I make this a priority, a new priority takes its place."

- "I can't get cooperation from the accounting department."

- "I never get around to making the calls I need to make to move this thing along."

- "Sue and Fred constantly argue at the committee meetings and ignore my facilitating."

The leader needs to be aware, however, that he may uncover more than his employee's ingrained pattern. There may be some **organizational alignment issues** present as well. In other words, he needs to check to see whether roles are well defined and executed in this particular project. Close-in coaching gives the leader a chance to check whether his staff is aligned or misaligned.

As you work with the executive on his coaching of staff, you can help him be thorough in attending to the boundaries and responsibilities of the roles of sponsor, agent, implementer, and advocate. Such attention can guide the thinking of the leader and employee so they can determine the best course of action.

For example, the employee may have surfaced a core role confusion in Sue and Fred's arguing that she cannot resolve because it is the sponsor's call to resolve. With this new information, the leader can clear up an issue fairly quickly with Sue and Fred by distinguishing between their roles on a particular project. They can then act more productively in the meetings.

The leader encourages the employee's initiative in planning for the action. In the previous example with Fred and Sue—when they argue—the executive can see how the employee decides what should come first: whether to get the leader involved in clearing up roles, or whether to facilitate the conflict in a problem-solving activity, or keep to the agenda in the meeting so it doesn't get side-tracked. The employee's development level increases when she first wrestles with which direction to go and then gets the leader's input on the priority action to take.

There are many opportunities for an executive to **use immediacy** in coaching an employee. The leader gives feedback on his experience of her here and now, as an example of the very thing the employee struggles with around the business goal. In the Sue and Fred example, the leader might use immediacy by saying, "You know, I'm finding it difficult to follow your agenda while we're talking. You seem unfocused as to where you need help. I wonder if Sue and Fred experience your facilitating in the same way—somewhat disjointed." This conversation invites the employee to see her own pattern of behaving that may be getting in the way. Instead of problem-solving the situation, the executive helps build ownership in the employee for finding solutions.

This is the core issue about coaching as a boss. Rather than advice-giving, it is a staff development activity. The leader conveys his belief that the employee has her own internal resources to solve the problem. To act on this belief is not to impose help but to give it when needed. This does not prevent the leader from stating his own positions, but instead of giving answers, he shares his viewpoint to provoke and expand his employee's thinking about the issue.

The leader may need to be directive if the employee does in fact need to increase her skill level. I am referring to an *attitude* that the leader holds: The employee is ultimately responsible for producing the results the leader has set for her. The executive provides the directive activities when needed, while encouraging the employee to increase her independence from his advice and direction.

Live-Action Coaching

What? Live-action coaching from a manager? Wouldn't that be a little strange? Actually, leaders do live-action coaching all the time. It has been called "management by walking around," and "supervising on the floor." Most of the time, the leader is not **clear about the structure of that coaching—how much on-the-spot intervening will occur.** If leader and employee do not talk about it beforehand, the employee may be waiting for the executive to intervene when the leader wants to see the employee work out a dilemma herself.

Or an employee may want a hands-off approach from the leader so she can learn from her own errors. The leader and employee need to reach an agreement about the live-action continuum—from observer to stop-action intervener.

Another agreement about the leader's intervention is particularly critical if the employee is a supervisor and leads meetings where the live-action coaching may occur. The executive and the supervisor also need to **decide whether or when the executive will step out of a coaching role and act within his authority as the manager.**

For instance, the supervisor may hold a team meeting where an issue comes up normally requiring the executive's input or decision. If the executive intervenes as manager without clarifying his role switch from coach to manager, the change can disrupt the group and undermine the supervisor's legitimate authority. The group may begin to distrust the executive's on-the-spot coaching and assume that everything he says comes from his position of authority when he does not intend that at all.

When the executive preemptively acts as the boss, the supervisor misses an opportunity to decide when it is best to turn to her manager for input on decisions. That moment is lost if the executive jumps in. He misses the chance to observe the supervisor's maturity in managing the boundary line between the executive's authority, the supervisor's authority, and the team's authority.

But what if the executive sees red flags in the supervisor's meeting? What if he knows the supervisor is giving incorrect information or is overstepping her authority? The executive can take action but should avoid undermining the supervisor in front of her employees. They can arrange beforehand under what conditions he will intervene as her boss and how he will do it. You can give some of the following suggestions to the executive about this agreement:

- During the meeting, wait a short time after you are inclined to intervene. Give the supervisor a chance to self-correct.

- Address the supervisor first, rather than talking immediately to her team. You can do this respectfully in front of the team. For example, you could say, "Jane, I have some information that is different from what you just gave, and I believe it would be useful here in the meeting."

- Be clear with the supervisor and the group that you are temporarily switching hats from the coach role to the boss role—"I'm switching hats from coach to boss at this point because there is some important information I want to add from my manager position." Then be clear when you are switching back to coach.

Once the executive learns to manage the boss-coach boundary during live-action coaching sessions, he turns his attention to the actual coaching itself. The guidelines for this are the same as those in Chapter Seven. As coach, the executive works to follow the employee's goals, foster changes in the employee's patterns of interaction, and help the employee maintain effective alignment in her organization.

Debriefing

Realistically, when a manager gives coaching feedback to an employee, it is evaluation, not "just feedback." Helping the executive understand this can develop him into a more effective manager. It is not possible for a leader to split his awareness of an employee into two areas, a "this is just feedback" area and a "this is how I judge your performance" area. He uses any experience of the employee on the job as material for evaluation. It is best when the leader is honest with himself about this, rather than trying unsuccessfully to split his experience of an employee, or reassuring the employee that he can engineer such a split.

When it comes to the **leader debriefing with the employee around her effectiveness,** many of the debriefing activities of executive coaching come into play with the employee self-assessing first. Discussions of the employee's strengths, challenges, patterns, management of alignment issues, and next steps can catapult the employee to the next level of proficiency.

When **the executive debriefs** *his* **effectiveness with the employee,** he needs to be honest about how much he wants to receive feedback on his coaching. Encourage him to be as open as possible. It may be difficult for an employee to give her manager an honest evaluation of his effectiveness as a coach. Therefore, **the executive needs to set an inviting tone** in order to get useful feedback. This is the one case where it is effective for **the coach to self-assess first** so the employee experiences the manager's readiness to receive real feedback. True openness means that the executive weighs what the employee says rather than assuming the information is either not useful or a reflection on the employee's performance. ("Of course I wasn't successful as your coach because you were such a lousy coachee!")

The following are some questions the leader can ask both himself and the employee during debriefing about his effectiveness:

- Did I stick to our contract?

- Was I clear in my roles, stating my parameters as your boss as well as helping you as your coach?

- What are examples of times I was successful and times I was not?

- Can we identify any patterns that I got into with you during this coaching that are typical of how we relate to each other?

- Which ones worked and which didn't?

- Of the ones that didn't work, what can I/we do about them?

- What do you/we want to strengthen or change as I coach you in the future?

When the executive coaches team members effectively, it has a ripple effect throughout the organization. Many of his other initiatives go more smoothly.

· · · · · · ·

CHAPTER TEN HIGHLIGHTS

Role Clarity

1. Help leaders manage the complexity created by the dual role of a boss-coach.
2. Coach leaders to accomplish the separate and sequential activities of Task 1 and Task 2.

Task 1: Name Performance Expectations and Ensure Employee Commitment

1. Help the leader set behaviorally specific expectations
2. Task 1 is complete when the employee
   - Understands business goals and outcomes.
   - Is committed to achieving the results.
   - Takes initiative in addressing the issues by using own ideas.

Coach the Leader to Deal with Resistance That Hinders the Completion of Task 1: Identify the Kind of Resistance and Brainstorm Ways to Deal with It

1. Lack of skill or competence
   - Provide appropriate direction and support.
   - Apply Situational Leadership Model.
   - Train if necessary.
2. Legitimate concern about organizational obstacles
   - Listen and respond to their loyal resistance.

3. Unproductive leader-employee pattern

- Identify an unproductive manager-employee pattern and change the manager's side of the pattern.
- Clearly state the goal and outcomes.
- Stay the course through the storm.
- Reinforce the change in the employee's side of the pattern, when it comes.

Task 2: Coaching for Increased Performance

1. The leader contracts with the employee

- Becomes familiar with the employee's challenges.
- Helps the employee get more specific about the issue.

2. The leader plans with the employee

- Identifies patterns.
- Identifies next step.
- Checks organizational alignment.
- Uses immediacy.

3. The leader coaches employee in live action (if needed)

- Provides clarity about their agreement of how much and what kind of on-the-spot intervention will occur.
- Is clear when the coach transitions from the coach's role into the role of boss.

4. The leader debriefs with the employee

- When evaluating employee effectiveness (1) realizes feedback to employee is evaluation; (2) debriefs employee's strengths, challenges, patterns, management of organizational alignment, next steps.
- When evaluating coach effectiveness (1) sets a tone of openness to receiving feedback; (2) self-assesses first, then asks for employee's feedback on his coaching.

· · · · · · ·

Afterword

. . . .

Now is the time to come full circle. One of the best ways that coaches can stay effective in their role is to receive coaching themselves. Can it be any other way? Everyone needs help to stay on track in the powerful interactional fields of organizations. As I have emphasized throughout the book, coaches have not reached such an evolved state that they are immune to these forces.

I stay on track two ways. First, I often do organizational consulting work in pairs; one of us is in the lead position and the other is in a secondary position. Two pairs of eyes see differently than one. By virtue of the position, the lead coach feels the wind resistance of being pulled into the leader's anxiety triangle. A telltale symptom is the loss of balanced backbone and heart work with her client. The second consultant—in a less anxious position—can see the systems patterns more easily, notice gaps in the process, and assist the lead to do a thorough job, bringing backbone and heart work back into balance.

Notice that I say "by virtue of the position"—a systems way of looking at how one person can function differently given different contexts. I have played both lead and second roles, sometimes in the same organization. I can feel my anxiety shift, as well as my ability to see peripherally, as I change from one position to the other. I also work with colleagues who seem quite calm in the second position and then lose some of their creativity as they shift to the lead.

I have learned not to personalize these shifts as signs of decreasing competence. They are a function more of position in the system rather than of identity. These differences in anxiety and clear seeing *by position* have been very instructional, reminding me what my clients go through when they experience the stress of the leadership position.

Therefore, a second way I keep my bearings is maintaining access to my own coach when I work alone in an organization. This coach is often a colleague who knows me well and consults with me behind the scenes to plan for a coaching session or debrief an experience I have with a client.

I used to think my need for a coach would diminish once I had worked with numerous clients and had many years under by belt. Twenty years and over a hundred clients later, my effectiveness has dramatically increased, but my desire to use a coach myself has remained high. I no longer see using a coach as a sign of incompetence but as a smart investment. Thank goodness, since that is what I tell my clients!

Perhaps I should say, *intellectually* I no longer see my requirement for a coach as a weakness. There are still times when I get embarrassed about my need for coaching when I am anxious about a client. I have learned that this is a sign of how really stuck I am in my own reactive vortex. I take my first step out when I turn to a colleague for coaching. Once I get clear and find my own bearings, I again see the importance of getting the coaching I need. The more I open myself to being coached, the more I know in my bones what my clients experience.

Appendix 1: Assessing Your Coaching Effectiveness

. . . .

You can develop your coaching skills more quickly when you take time to evaluate each of your coaching sessions and plan for the next one. Following are assessment sheets you can use for a quick check of how you did. Occasionally, you may want to have your client fill them out on you to initiate feedback. The forms list the foundational skills that undergird the four coaching phases.

Coaching Assessment

Contracting

To what extent did you
(*1 is low, 5 is high*)

Listen, follow your natural curiosity.

1	2	3	4	5

Show that you understood the client's core concerns.

1	2	3	4	5

Give feedback—your immediate, here-and-now experience of the other person.

1	2	3	4	5

Help the client identify measurable goals.

1	2	3	4	5

Planning

To what extent did you:
(*1 is low, 5 is high*)

Help the client identify a specific next step.

| 1 | 2 | 3 | 4 | 5 |

Focus the leader on the pattern she needs to change.

| 1 | 2 | 3 | 4 | 5 |

Ensure the leader's strategy works toward the alignment of roles.

| 1 | 2 | 3 | 4 | 5 |

Help the leader plan creatively for the push-back to the change.

| 1 | 2 | 3 | 4 | 5 |

Live-Action Coaching

To what extent did you:
(1 is low, 5 is high)

Ensure everyone involved understood the structure of the session and that your role was well-sponsored.

1	2	3	4	5

Follow the client's goals (stay active *and* stay out of the way).

1	2	3	4	5

Foster pattern breaking for more effective action on the part of the client.

1	2	3	4	5

Focus on patterns that strengthen the leader's effectiveness in his role.

1	2	3	4	5

Debriefing

To what extent did you:
(1 is low, 5 is high)

Encourage the client to self-assess her strengths, challenges, central patterns, and role alignment.

1	2	3	4	5

Give your client your feedback, both supportive and challenging.

1	2	3	4	5

Help the leader plan her next step.

1	2	3	4	5

Invite the client to give you feedback on your coaching.

1	2	3	4	5

Appendix 2: Questions for Clients

. . . .

Included in this appendix are examples of questions that you can ask your clients at various stages throughout the coaching process. You will recognize them as the questions that are embedded throughout the chapters and stories of this book. They are not meant as a prescription or recipe for engagement with executives. They are intended as a stimulus to your thinking when approaching your clients.

The goal behind all of these questions is raising ownership and resilience in your client. Use whichever ones you find helpful to get you started in the conversation. Ultimately, you will create your own questions for engaging both your resourcefulness and the resilience of the leaders with whom you work.

Contracting

What business challenges are you facing?

Have you met this challenge successfully before?*

What is your best thinking about this issue?*

Note: Questions marked with an asterisk are excerpted, adapted, and used with the permission of Rob Schachter, from "Questions When Contracting with Leaders," unpublished document, 1997.

What are the gaps in meeting the same kind of challenge this time?*

What is keeping you from getting the results you want?

How do you account for not being able to accomplish this?*

How have you responded to this issue?

Do you have any sense of your part in not meeting the challenge this time?*

How urgent are you?*

How much time do you have to achieve this?

What do you find personally challenging about leading this effort, given the results you have to date?*

How do you think I could be useful to you?

Do you have the authority to sponsor this plan, or do you need sponsorship from someone else?

Goals

What do you want to accomplish in this effort?*

What outcomes do you want?*

What would be achievable results and what would be the specific timeframe?*

What would successfully fulfilling those goals look like? How would you measure it?

What is your best thinking about this issue?*

What behaviors need to be different in team members to accomplish the results?

In your position as leader, what challenges do you personally feel in pulling this off?*

What behaviors will you need to enhance or change?

How does this challenge fit into goals you have for yourself?

To what extent do the people who report to you hold the same perspective or urgency that you have?*

Does your team know as much about what you're thinking as I know now?*

Planning

How clear have you been with your team so they understand you stand behind this challenge?

What do you know and what don't you know? Can you be clear about both? What information and support do you need and from whom?

How do you want to increase participation within the work group?

How clear have you been in your performance expectations?

Are these expectations compromised in some way by the surrounding context?

Are matrixed groups clear about their roles on this issue? Do they know to whom they are accountable and for which items?

Are you the decision maker? Which decisions will you make and which will you delegate?

What strengths do you have as a leader that you want to preserve and build upon?

Patterns

What pattern are you playing out with the other person? Is the pattern effective? If not, how does it detract from your success?

What does the other person do or not do that triggers your response? Does this interaction have a familiar ring to it? Can you count on people (yourself included) to react in familiar ways? Is this so recurring that you could "Name That Tune"? How would it be identified as a news headline?

How do you encourage others to keep doing the things you don't like? What is your contribution to this pattern? What do you do that starts them down that path in the first place?

What pulls you off course?

What can you do to stay on course? And then what can you do when that doesn't work? And then what can you do?

Boundaries

Do people know what is expected of them?

What are the boundaries of this system?

Are they frequently compromised so that work is difficult to do?

Are they so rigid that people are not getting essential information and resources from other parts of the organization?

Debriefing

How do you think you did?

To what extent did you achieve your goal? What did you do well?

Did you follow the mandate of your role as sponsor, implementer, advocate, or agent?

Did you match your managing style to the developmental need of the employee?

Did you establish a pattern that enhanced the interaction?

What internal cues can you identify when you get into this pattern (either for one that works or one that does not work)?

What loose ends around decision making, participation, and so forth need to be clarified?

What challenges do you continue to face?

What next step do you want to take?

What do you want to strengthen or change as I coach you in the future?

Appendix 3: Combining Coaching and Consulting for Powerful Results

. . . .

*E*xecutive Coaching with Backbone and Heart* has detailed the methods and skills involved in coaching leaders. I've focused largely on the one-on-one relationship between the coach and the executive. While Chapter Nine is addressed to consultants who want to develop a larger coaching practice, Appendix 3 provides ideas for coaches doing one-on-one work who want to move into larger organizational change efforts. Your clients may request your assistance in larger change agent arenas, wanting you to join them in the live-action work of their organizations.

Most of the coaching I do occurs in a larger partnership with the executive concerning an organizational initiative she launches. Since consulting and coaching are mutually reinforcing, the leader's efforts benefit from such a powerful combination. The consulting process allows the executive to have an impact on a larger part of the organization in a shorter time. In addition, the coaching deepens the executive's commitment to sustain her change goals and outcomes. Any effective consultation process includes ongoing coaching as an integral part of the work and can make significant contributions to organizations.

These gains result when the leader strongly sponsors the executive coaching and other organizational change efforts. Then the coach-consultant can intervene on multiple levels in the company by using many change agent roles: interviewing, facilitating, training, coaching of other managers in the system, and so forth.

Ongoing coaching of the executive empowers these extensive organizational efforts.

Before discussing how coaching and consulting can be combined, I will talk briefly about the results of such an undertaking. They highlight the benefits of offering a fuller set of services to executives.

The Client's Business Results

Following are actual results clients have achieved during executive coaching processes that link executive coaching with larger consulting interventions in the executive's company:

From a bottom rank on market share in the company

> *to* the top rank (bottom-line goal).

From the lowest production level

> *to* the highest production in the company (bottom-line goal).

From no department connecting its work to the organization's bottom-line goals

> *to* every department organized to deliver on the three major goals of the company. This change resulted in sustaining membership in the "top three" rating of a customer satisfaction index (work-process goal, leading to bottom-line outcome).

From an HR department delivering basic personnel benefits and policies

> *to* becoming a full-service HR department linking organization development work with personnel delivery (work-process goal).

From leaders being protected from hearing the "bad news" from peers and direct reports

> *to* getting consistently "straight" feedback from peers and direct reports across the company (human relations goal).

From strained combative management-union relationships

to union-management collaboration on significant business decisions (human relations goal).

Your Contribution to Leaders' Business Results

There is often the question of how much credit the coach-consultant can take for achieving business results. How does a change agent measure his work? The answers are simple and complex. If the executive who received coaching is getting higher results, who achieved the outcomes? The client! Is the executive coaching a critical factor? Yes! More difficult questions deal with the specific difference or contribution that the coaching-consulting makes to the results.

The two extreme answers, of course, are to take no credit or to take all of it. Taking none fails to respect the coaching-consulting process—or it may be a symptom of the change agent not paying attention to the business results of the client. Walking away with all or most of the credit grabs the responsibility for results away from the client, a symptom of Rescue Model work.

Actually, the client is fundamentally accountable for her results, *and* the partnership of the executive coaching process significantly affects those results. The best person to answer *how* the coaching-consulting influenced the organization is the *client*. If the coaching is successful, it is the client who shows distinctly new behaviors and can tell you to what extent those changes were due to the coaching.

Because the executive coach is a business partner, it is his responsibility to ensure that the coaching conversations stay relevant to those results. Therefore, he should be asking the leader to define how the process helps the leader achieve her goals. This serves two purposes: (1) keeping the change agent work relevant and on track, and (2) building and sustaining credibility for the coaching-consulting process. The more the client can articulate the connection in specific ways, the more substantial the business partnership becomes. You no longer have the sole burden of proving your worth to the business of the organization. Instead you collect information on the specific contribution the coaching-consulting makes to a particular process.

Given *what* can be accomplished by a consulting-coaching effort, let's turn to *how* it is done.

Combining Coaching and Consulting

There are numerous approaches to creating organizational change. Surveying the theory and process of organization consulting is beyond the scope of this book.[1] Following, however, is a sample of how putting consulting and coaching together can produce powerful results. At LIOS Consulting Corporation we take an approach that employs such a combination. The five tenets that underlie this work are as follows:

Keep business results and human processes linked.

Encourage and stimulate a stronger relationship between the leader and the work group, including the ability to manage productive conflict.

Build the leadership capabilities of the executive, particularly articulating positions clearly (backbone) and staying in strong relationship with the group (heart).

Develop individuals within the work group to bring their own leadership forward, taking initiatives that involve productive collaboration and challenge.

Provide live-action interventions while the team is conducting real work.

Encouraging the interplay of these factors between a leader and a work group produces the powerful results listed above.

Here are some of the consulting activities that, with strong sponsorship from the leader, can contribute to this productive dynamic. Notice the classic blend of consultation with coaching. Effective outcomes result when you work this traditional blend along with a systems perspective to surface, identify, enhance, or change the strong patterns operating in the leader and the team arising from their co-created interactional field. Many moments of individual discovery and behavioral change create the possibility of a team shift to greater effectiveness. The consulting process is listed along with the companion coaching activity.

Change Agent Activities

- Contract with executives for work with them and their immediate team.

  Coach the leader during the contracting process.

- Conduct individual interviews of team members.

  Coach individuals to identify specific goals to increase their own effectiveness.

- Hold business meetings, facilitated by the leader, to address actual organizational issues. Provide just-in-time training of models that develop crisper visions, goals, decisions, and action plans regarding the business issues.

  Coach the leader and the group in their sessions while they conduct their business.

  Coach the leader in debrief and planning sessions between meetings.

- Train the leader and the team in interactional skills to develop their resources in surfacing information, managing conflict, and making decisions.

  Coach individuals during training sessions.

  Coach during debriefing.

- Identify staff and operations areas of the organization that need further development.

  Coach leader to build sustaining sponsorship across the organization.

  Coach executive during meetings they lead with sustaining sponsors.

  Coach leader to ensure successful project management implementation across the organization.

  Coach designated leaders in the organization who have a high impact on the business.

- Train designated executives to become more effective coaches of their direct reports.

  Coach leaders as needed.

- Train an internal group to become coaches and continuing change agents in the organization.

  Coach these individuals as needed.

A range of skills is required to do the activities catalogued above. The following list of competencies gives you a sense of what is necessary to expand your practice to include a blend of coaching with consulting.

Consultant Competencies

Although one-on-one coaches need to have many of the competencies listed here, consultants need to master all of them. They work on larger processes, ones that often affect a whole department, division, or the entire company. They intervene in multiple arenas simultaneously. Consultants play the other roles listed here that include and go beyond coaching; for example, project manager, trainer, and meeting facilitator.

There is a great deal of overlap between these skills and the management competencies cited in Chapter Eight. When it comes to enhancing people's performance at work, executives and consultants share much of the same people skill requirements, though they use them in distinctly different roles. You can use the list to assess the range and depth of your current change agent skills.

Consultant Competencies

Systems functioning	Expands awareness of presenting issues to include (1) the systemic patterns at play, (2) the function of the organization's infrastructure, (3) the emotional process underlying organizational issues, and (4) the larger community that undergirds the organization.
	Includes self in the reciprocity of interactions.
	Works to increase own and others' resilience in functioning within the system and among systems.
Strengthening sustaining sponsorship	Educates and coaches leaders in critical dimensions of sponsorship.
	Ensures role clarity between sponsors and change agents.
	Declines duties that undermine the relationships and responsibilities sponsors and implementers have to one another.
Project managing	Educates and coaches leaders to (1) give specific direction and identify key roles, responsibilities, and timeframes for

projects, (2) allocate the people to resource each project, (3) identify the decision makers, (4) clarify the single point agent for project, and (5) sponsor the kick-off.

Acts as single point agent in designated projects to monitor processes and ensures that the leaders sustain cross-functional sponsorship.

Facilitating meetings	Leads meetings effectively.
	Develops an agenda, prioritizing items for best use of time.
	Facilitates discussion to gain maximum participation.
	Helps group members identify key needs, ideas, and plans for action.
	Uses a variety of group process methods to achieve effective engagement, leading to synergistic results and productive outcomes.
Decision making	Takes responsibility for clarity around who makes decisions.
	Uses several decision styles effectively; for example, consultative, delegation, consensus.
	When in the decision-maker role, can firmly say yes or no and stay connected with constituents.
Promoting conversations	Clarifies the parameters of discussions to maximize their effectiveness.

Helps all constituencies be heard and speak to each other directly.

Seeks to surface information and break habitual thinking.

Addresses underlying issues. Talks about the tough issues.

Takes a learning stance in conversations.

Coaching

Promotes leadership and initiative in people across all roles in the organization.

Gives specific feedback to others about their strengths and weaknesses, building competence and commitment in others.

Helps people clarify their positions and stay connected in their work relationships.

Training

Designs and delivers training linked to strategic organizational goals.

Engages participants while achieving the intended training objectives.

Is capable of facilitating knowledge, attitude, and skill training. Provides clear theory sessions.

Gives easy-to-follow instructions for skill practice.

Advocating

Effectively advocates for own ideas and one's part of the organization.

Uses advocacy to enhance the broader strategic vision of the whole organization. Communicates understanding and

	commitment to the larger goals when advocating.
Strategic thinking	Understands the whole picture. Sees complex functions from the perspective of the whole.
	Can weigh external and internal factors that affect the organization's productivity and results. Comprehends business issues and how an organization works.
Cultivating customer	Perceives the customer–vendor–relationships internal customer (employee)–larger community (civic contexts) relationships as mutually reinforcing.
	Works to streamline processes to aid these relationships.
Visioning	Develops a clear vision for oneself and one's part of the organization.
	Identifies specific and measurable goals (which are challenging, bracing, a stretch) to achieve the vision, and communicates the vision and goals effectively.
	Engages constituents in conversations to further the vision, gain greater clarity, and increase communal commitment.
	Helps leaders do the same in the organization.

Notes

· ·

Chapter One

1. Even the image of a nested set of spheres is too confining to connote, among other things, the fluidity of interconnecting systems. To indicate the sensitivity of any system's sphere of influence to the activities in other systems, I have added the image of the web with its strength and responsiveness to changes. Imagine the web intersecting through all the spheres.

Chapter Two

1. A colleague of mine, Rob Schachter, says, "Take the bull by the horns and then hand it back to them." It applies to those delicate times that call for both bold initiative *and* following a client's lead simultaneously.

2. This term was first defined by Murray Bowen and later used by Edwin Friedman. I give it only the barest definition here. For an accessible introduction to the journey of self-differentiation, see Friedman (1985) and Kerr and Bowen (1988).

3. One path that can lead to greater mastery is called Family of Origin work. Since it is a developmental therapeutic process, it is beyond the scope of this book. For those interested in Family of Origin work, see Gilbert (1992) and Richardson (1984). For a related Family of Origin resource with the distinctive exploration of personal authority, see Williamson (1991).

4. The interplay of order and chaos and the experience of ambiguity and confusion mentioned here give a cursory explanation of an approach to organizations that is informed by the new science in biology and physics. For an accessible introduction, see Wheatley (1992).

5. See Footnote 3. Also, for brain research on reactivity, see Goleman (1995).

Chapter Three

1. I am fortunate to be in constant conversation with my colleagues at the Leadership Institute of Seattle (LIOS) at Bastyr University and at LIOS Consulting Corporation. Many of the key systems theoretical assumptions I bring to coaching and successful change are also shared and used by them in their work.

2. I use the terms *interactional force field* or *social interactional field* because they are conducive to a work environment. The actual term used in the discipline of family systems is *emotional field*. For a more in-depth development of the term, see Kerr and Bowen (1988).

3. See Note 3 from Chapter Two.

4. My introduction to pattern thinking was through Ronald Short (1985a, 1985b), a former director of the Leadership Institute of Seattle (LIOS). Short studied with Salvador Minuchin (1974) and found a way to apply Minuchin's structural systems thinking to organizations.

Chapter Four

1. These and other questions to better understand patterns are listed in Appendix Two.

Chapter Five

1. I find it useful to think of a guiding motto for each of the phases. I list them in each of the phase subtitles.

2. For an excellent introduction to action research, see Block (1981). Another coaching approach that draws from the stages of action

research (in broad brush strokes) can be found in Dotlich and Cairo (1999).

3. You may notice that the action research step of data collection seems to be missing from the coaching phases. Actually, it is embedded in all four of them. Many of the data are in the coach's direct experience of leaders as they go through these phases. That is why I find it useful to experience leaders within their settings at some point, and to observe how they interact with their teams (Chapter Seven). In a sense, I am collecting information on how leaders collect data and receive feedback about themselves and the business issues.

4. These are some of the listening skills that Carkhuff (1969), drawing from Carl Rogers, defines in working with clients to help them solve their own problems. Carkhuff gives technical definitions to the skills that differ from normal cultural use, particularly *confrontation* and *respect*.

Appendix Three

1. For further resources, see Lippitt and Lippitt (1986), Schein (1987, 1988), Bunker and Alban (1997), and Weisbord (1987).

References

Bell, Chip R. *Managers as Mentors*. San Francisco: Berrett-Koehler, 1996.

Blanchard, K., Zigarmi, P., and Zigarmi, D. *Leadership and the One Minute Manager*. New York: William Morrow, 1985.

Block, P. *Flawless Consulting*. San Diego: University Associates, 1981.(Second edition, San Francisco: Jossey-Bass, 1999.)

Bunker, B., and Alban, B. *Large Group Interventions*. San Francisco: Jossey-Bass, 1997.

Carkhuff, R. *Helping and Human Relations*. New York: Holt, 1969.

Conner, D. *Managing at the Speed of Change*. New York: Villard, 1993.

Crosby, R. *The Authentic Leader*. Seattle: Skaya, 1998.

Dotlich, D., and Cairo, P. *Action Coaching*. San Francisco: Jossey-Bass, 1999.

Fournies, F. *Coaching for Improved Work Performance*. New York: McGraw-Hill, 1998.

Friedman, E. *Generation to Generation*. New York: Guilford, 1985.

Gilbert, R. *Extraordinary Relationships*. Minneapolis: Chronimed, 1992.

Goleman, D. *Emotional Intelligence*. New York: Bantam Books, 1995.

Hargrove, R. *Masterful Coaching*. San Diego: Pfeiffer, 1995.

Kerr, M., and Bowen, M. *Family Evaluation*. New York: Norton, 1988.

Kinlaw, D. *Coaching for Commitment*. San Diego: Pfeiffer, 1993. (Second edition, San Francisco: Jossey-Bass, 1999.)

Lippitt, G., and Lippitt, R. *The Consulting Process in Action*. San Diego: Pfeiffer, 1986.

Minuchin, S. *Families and Family Therapy*. Cambridge: Harvard University Press, 1974.

Richardson, R. *Family Ties that Bind*. Vancouver, B.C., Canada: Self-Counsel Press, 1984.

Schachter, R. "Questions When Contracting with Leaders." Unpublished document, 1997. LIOS Consulting Corporation.

Schein, E. *Process Consultation*, vol. 1, 2nd edition. Reading, Mass.: Addison-Wesley, 1988.

Schein, E. *Process Consultation: Lessons for Managers and Consultants*, vol. 2, 1st edition. Reading, Mass.: Addison-Wesley, 1987.

Senge, P. *The Fifth Discipline*. New York: Doubleday Currency, 1990.

Short, R. "Structural Family Therapy and Consultative Practice: A Paradigm Shift for OD." *Consultation, an International Journal*, Summer, 1985a, 4(2), 1–17.

Short, R. "Structural Family Therapy and Consultative Practice: A Paradigm Shift for OD." *Consultation, an International Journal*, Fall, 1985b, 4(3), 1–12.

Weisbord, M. *Productive Workplaces*. San Francisco: Jossey-Bass, 1987.

Wheatley, M. *Leadership and the New Science*. San Francisco: Berrett-Koehler, 1992.

Whitmore, J. *Coaching for Performance*. 2nd edition. London: Nicholas Brealey, 1996.

Whitworth, L., Kimsey-House, H., and Sandahl, P. *Co-Active Coaching*. Palo Alto: Davies-Black, 1998.

Williamson, D. *The Intimacy Paradox*. New York: Guilford Press, 1991.

Index